Turpin Times

An Illini Sports Scrapbook

By
Jim Turpin

Sports Publishing L.L.C.
www.sportspublishingllc.com

Project manager/Photo insert design: Jim Henehan
Director of production: Susan M. Moyer
Dust jacket design: Kenneth J. O'Brien
Developmental Editor: Stephanie Fuqua
Copy Editor: Cindy McNew

ISBN: 1-58261-445-8

Printed in the United States of America

Sports Publishing L.L.C.
www.sportspublishingllc.com

Dedication

To my wife, Louise, who has put up with a lot. I love you.

To my children and their spouses: Chris and Jim, Dan and Christine, Jayne and Joe, you make me so proud. I realize more with each passing day that my family is everything.

To my grandchildren: Carly, Kendall, Shayne, Quinn, Jenna, and Jordan. Someday you may read this and know how Papa spent most of his life. I hope the book will bring you as much joy as this life has brought me. God bless.

———————————————————

Contents

Introduction

One of the most difficult decisions a person has to make is when to quit. After more than thirty years of broadcasting play-by-play for the University of Illinois football and basketball teams, I still feel quite capable of performing my duties at a very high level. Obviously, others' opinions may differ.

Ron Guenther, University of Illinois athletic director, called a meeting in his office to discuss my future as Illinois' play-by-play announcer. Present at the meeting were John Foreman and I. Foreman is editor and general manager of *The Champaign-Urbana News-Gazette* and was overseeing the operation of radio stations WDWS and WHMS in Champaign. I have been employed by those stations, in various capacities, since 1980.

At that meeting, Guenther asked me how much longer I intended to do the play-by-play. He explained that he is always planning ahead, always looking down the road a few years, particularly with regard to personnel.

I wanted to reply, "For as long as I'm healthy and capable," but I knew that wouldn't fly. He wanted me to be a little more specific. Having never been fired from a job and being uncertain as to what Guenther had in mind, I picked "three more years" out of the air. He agreed to that. Guenther, Foreman and I shook hands on the deal, and that was that. My play-by-play duties would end at the conclusion of the 2001-2002 basketball season.

I don't know why I said "three more years" and not "five more years," or "ten more years," but deep down I knew that three was about the maximum the AD would permit. I would be seventy years old by then, and, I hoped, still able to do a good job. Being remembered as one who retired at the top of his game and not as one who stayed around too long was important to me.

As the final year approached, the management of WDWS and WHMS (primarily General Manager Steve Khachaturian) set out to make sure that my replacement came from the WDWS staff and not from Chicago or some other market. He selected Brian Barnhart, who had just recently moved back to the area after a stint broadcasting baseball for the Anaheim Angels.

Barnhart had impressive "pipes," and several members of Guenther's staff liked the way he sounded on the air. Khachaturian and Foreman structured a deal for Barnhart that would ensure he would still be on board when my three years were up. This included doing the early morning news on WDWS, plus some play-by-play for other Illini sports, including baseball. As it turned out, Brian was able to fill in for me on some Illini football and basketball broadcasts during the 2001-2002 season when I had conflicts or was ill.

Dave Loane, who had been waiting in the wings for thirteen years in hopes of being my successor, was able to make alternate plans, which included doing volleyball and women's basketball broadcasts for Fox TV as well as Illini women's games and Illini baseball on WDWS.

So everyone was happy. Sort of.

In part, this book is about that final year. It contains, in some detail, what happened on and off the field and court to Ron Turner's football team and Bill Self's basketball team.

In addition, the book contains flashbacks–my recollections of things that happened in the past as I covered the Illini for more than thirty years. A bus ride, a shoot-around, a practice session, a hotel, an airport, a plane ride, a restaurant, a hospital, a conversation, a game, a face in the crowd often reminded me of games and seasons past. And more importantly, they were reminders of the coaches and players who took part.

It has been a wonderful ride. I shall be eternally grateful to Mrs. Marajen Stevick Chinigo, the owner of *The News-Gazette* and WDWS/WHMS, who hired me in 1980 and let me do my job. She takes great pride in being the sole local owner of a newspaper and two radio stations in this era of mergers and out-of-town ownership. I take great pride in working for her.

Chapter 1

How It All Began

It was the summer of 1938. The University of Illinois and Notre Dame had battled to an epic 0-0 tie the previous October. Pitcher Ray Poat compiled a perfect 10-0 record with the Illini baseball team. Pick Dehner tied the Big Ten basketball scoring record with twenty-nine points against the University of Chicago. Hek Kenney, who would later have a gym named after him, compiled amazing records in wrestling. And on a dusty street where ramshackle houses teetered side by side and working men and women sought front porches to escape the scorching heat, a play-by-play announcer's career began. I was six years old.

The address was 127 East Lafayette in Olney, Illinois, the home of the white squirrels. In the side yard, my cousin Ronnie Hockman and I re-created some of the greatest baseball games ever played. Just the two of us. A broomstick for a bat. A tennis ball to hit. And an elaborate spiral-bound notebook where we kept the box scores and the records.

One of us would pitch; the other would bat. I might be the Cardinals and he the Yankees. Or the Cubs and the Tigers. Anything hit on the ground was an out. A ball hit to the edge of the street was a single; to the middle of the street was a double.

A shot off the house of our neighbor across the street was a triple. Over the house was a home run. The neighbor's name was Mrs. Miller: if she had a first name, I never knew it. She was a fortune teller.

So far, nothing special. Just two kids playing ball. Two barefooted kids wearing bib overalls and smacking the heck out of an old tennis ball with a dilapidated broomstick. But I did the play-by-play of every pitch of every game, whether I was pitching or batting.

I'd pitch and talk at the same time. I'd wind up: "Here's the windup, here's the pitch on the way." Ronnie would swing. If he missed, I'd shout, "Swung on and missed, he's outta there on strikes. That's three up and three down. Going into the bottom of the ninth, the Cards still lead five to two with the Yankees coming to bat." Then I'd take the broom and he'd pitch. And I would continue the play-by-play. It just about drove our parents and the neighbors nuts. Years later my Aunt John (Ronnie's mother) found the spiral notebook, and we all had a good laugh.

Could it be possible that a six-year-old boy knew at that age what he wanted to do as a profession? I've heard of young men and women knowing early on that they wanted to be doctors or lawyers, but play-by-play announcers? Relatively speaking, there aren't many play-by-play announcers out there. When Dick Vitale named me as one of sixteen play-by-play announcers on his "Sweet Sixteen All-Radio Team" in 2000, I felt honored. In college basketball there were more than 300 play-by-play announcers who didn't make Vitale's team, so it was nice to be included.

After we quit playing and announcing in the side yard, my play-by-play career went on hold for a number of years as I grew up and went through the Olney school system playing football, basketball, baseball, softball, and tennis. In smaller schools, most athletes played a number of sports. I did a little trash-talking as a high school athlete, but no play-by-play. In Junior Legion baseball I pitched back-to-back no-hitters against mighty St. Francisville and Oblong, but any play-by-play was under my breath.

In 1952 I was drafted into the U.S. Army, but a recent knee operation resulted in a nine-month deferment. I went back to Olney and got a part-time job at radio station WVLN. It was there that I first began doing play-by-play for real. I did high school football and basketball games live and on tape.

I was also able to do some news broadcasting, along with market reports, weather, DJ work, and emptying the waste cans. There is no substitute for working at a small station if a person is hoping to get into the radio business. One day, the sports director, Bert DeBarr, asked me if I wanted to help him broadcast the state high school basketball tournament. I almost fainted with joy. We were off to Huff Gym at the U of I!

When we began the broadcast of our first game of the tournament, I was so happy that I almost cried. Bert let me do every other game, and it was an exhausting and exciting experience. It would prove to be a launching pad for my career in broadcasting. I have always been grateful to Marshall Poole, the WVLN owner and manager who gave me a chance. He once said to me, "I could see it in your eyes. You really wanted this job. You really wanted to get into radio." Over the years I have interviewed dozens and dozens of young radio applicants: I have always remembered to look into their eyes. If it's there, you can see it. If a job was available, it didn't necessarily go to the one with the most talent at that point; it went to the one with that look. Hiring people that way is not very scientific, but it sure has worked for me.

When the nine-month deferment was up, Uncle Sam did not forget me. I went back into the draft and wound up as a dot-and-dash man. That's the Army term for a Morse code operator. After basic training and radio operator's school at Fort Riley, Kansas, I was assigned to Korea, where surprisingly enough, my play-by-play career would get another boost.

One day, while hunkered down in a tent amidst the snow and cold of the area around the demilitarized zone, I heard an announcer on the Armed Forces Korea Network say that the network was looking for announcers with radio experience to join the network.

"Radio experience? Hey, that's me! Surely you guys have heard of that blockbuster station in Olney, Illinois, WVLN!" I applied, and just a few weeks later I was on my way to the southernmost part of Korea, Pusan, to join Radio Station Homesteader. Homesteader was one of four stations on the AFKN. We fed stories to the Far East Network in Tokyo. The staff consisted of eight to ten enlisted men and one officer.

My main duty at Homesteader during the fifteen months I was there was to host an early morning show. Typical stuff: news, weather, sports, talk, and lots of music. I was a Robin Williams sort–Good Morning, Korea! I also wrote, produced, and narrated a weekly show called "This Is Jazz." A friend, Bill Brackett, and I put together a weird show called "The Purple Eye," which consisted of eerie music and some off-the-wall poetry that we wrote. GIs didn't quite know what to make of this show. Nor did we. But it was popular, and we liked doing it.

I was also part of a special events team that traveled around Korea interviewing visiting celebrities, members of USO shows, governmental officials, and interesting GIs. I did an interview with General James Van Fleet, who came to look for his son who was missing in action. I also did a pretty good one-on-one with Secretary of Defense Charles Wilson. But the most famous person I talked to was Marilyn Monroe. Marilyn had come to Korea to entertain the troops, and she was a smashing success! My interview with her lasted almost ten minutes. Up close, attired in army fatigues and boots, she was just about the most beautiful woman I had ever seen. Of course, I had been away from home for more than a year. Marilyn kept calling me "John" during the interview, but I didn't mind.

My big break came when the station decided to begin broadcasting several of the football, basketball, and baseball games that the GIs were playing all over Korea.

Luckily, I was the only person on staff who had any play-by-play experience. The brief stint at WVLN not only enabled me to get transferred to AFKN, but also allowed me to do dozens of games and get paid for it by Uncle Sam. What a country!

I came back to the United States in May of 1955 and enrolled at the University of Illinois. The GI Bill helped, but my wife Louise and I still needed to work. She worked in the office of Veteran's Housing under a wonderful man named Cal Shull, and I applied at WDWS in Champaign where Larry Stewart was the manager. My work at WVLN and AFKN made me one of the more experienced announcers walking in off the street, so Stewart hired me. The pay was $1 an hour, but Stewart promised I could work 35 hours a week. We were rich!

Part of my duties at WDWS consisted of doing play-by-play of high school football and basketball games. We broad-casted Urbana High School football games by looking out the window of the gymnasium. I developed a relationship with

Champaign coach Tommy Stewart and Urbana coach Warren Smith-two great coaches and gentlemen. In all my years I have never met a better pair. I loved them.

Doing high school games was a great experience for me, but I always envied Stewart who did play-by-play for the Illlini. He also did a two-hour talk show in the morning called "Penny for Your Thoughts." And, of course, he was in charge of everything as vice president and general manager of both the AM and FM stations. My goal was to someday have that job. I wanted to do all the things that he was doing. I thought that would be ideal; who could want more? That was in 1955. It took a while, but in November 1980, I reached my goal.

Section 1

FOOTBALL

Chapter 2

The Sugar Bowl

The rain continued to fall, as it had for the past forty-eight hours.

Across the street from the Superdome, a dozen yellow-slickered cops sat on their motorcycles. Some were to be a part of the police escort that would accompany the team buses back to the Hilton. Others stared straight ahead, hoping that the post-Sugar Bowl traffic jam would somehow clear up. Then they could go home. After all, it was past midnight. The game had been very long.

One bus, filled with friends and families of the coaches and players, began to roll. Several women, some with children in their arms, ran alongside the bus and pounded on the door, hoping to be let in. They too were anxious to get some place warm and dry so that the young kids could sleep. The game had indeed been very long.

But the bus driver ignored them, and they trudged back to where the rest of us were waiting, under the Superdome overhang. It was relatively dry there, but the fumes from the team buses were so strong that some of us were gagging.

The players began to file out of the Superdome and boarded the three team buses.

They looked so sad. Some were limping. A couple held ice packs on sore spots. They looked down as they walked, their dress shoes splashing through the puddles. They were hurting now, but not all the hurt was physical.

Greg McMahon, the Illini special teams coach, and I stood in the steady drizzle. We had watched the friends and families bus episode. Now we looked at the couple dozen people hugging the Superdome wall, hoping that another bus would arrive soon.

"This is what happens when you get beat," Greg said with a slight smile.

I smiled back at him. I wanted to say something. But as always, words are hard to come by after a defeat. Especially a defeat like this one. Later, when enough time has passed, it will be easier to talk about. And we will look back on the 2001 season with great joy and pride: an undisputed Big Ten championship and a trip to one of the four prized BCS games. But not tonight.

Harry Hiestand, the Illini offensive line coach, joined us.

"Your last football broadcast, right? Sorry we couldn't have made it better. But thanks for all that you have done for us over the years. We really appreciate it," he said.

I was stunned that Coach Hiestand would remember something like that just an hour or so after a hard defeat. He must have had a million things on his mind at that moment, but he was classy enough to congratulate me. I won't ever forget that. "Thank you, Coach," I said.

Minutes later, Harry led a charge of several of us out into the street where he commanded a bus driver to open the door and let us in. You don't mess with a tough offensive line coach. The door opened, and we poured in. We were finally on our way back to the hotel.

When we arrived at the Hilton about forty-five minutes later, a few people were waiting in the lobby. They applauded and yelled, "ILL - INI!" as the players walked by towards the elevators. It was a gallant effort on the part of the Illini fans, but a far cry from the enthusiastic, loud and energetic throng that had been there for the pregame pep rally several hours ago.

At 2 a.m. my wife and I were packing. Our bags needed to be ready for pickup by 6 a.m. for the flight back to Champaign. Once the bags were packed and the lights were out, I felt totally exhausted, yet I was unable to fall asleep.

Earlier that evening, Bob Asmussen, the Illini football writer for *The Champaign-Urbana News-Gazette*, had asked me to describe how I felt getting ready to do my last football broadcast. I told him truthfully that I didn't feel anything. I really hadn't given it much thought. And I had a basketball broadcast to do the next night back at the Assembly Hall. My only concern was to do a good broadcast and bring home a victory.

My broadcast colleagues, Brian Barnhart and Ed Bond, and I had taxied to the Superdome at 4:15 p.m. Brian was to take part in our local pregame show on WDWS/WHMS, called "Illini Game Day," which began at 5 p.m.

When we arrived, we found that the booth next to ours was to be occupied by the Illinois coaches. They had taped ugly gray towels to the side windows of their booth, presumably to keep us from stealing their secrets. We couldn't see them, they couldn't see us, and our engineer couldn't see the entire field because of the towels. We thought it was very funny. Once the game began, the coaches had to put up with LSU fans who were seated right in front of their booth; the Tiger fans turned around time after time to shout at the Illini coaches, especially when something went very right for LSU or very wrong for Illinois. That happened a lot during the first half.

Our booth had two levels. To get from the upper level, where the engineer and equipment were, to the lower level, where the broadcasters were, you had to climb down a steel-rung ladder. It reminded me of going into a submarine. Some of us were better at it than others. Our halftime guest, Big Ten Commissioner Jim Delaney, was undisputedly the most nimble. We were all quite surprised that there would be a booth of this sort in the grand Superdome.

Our broadcast team's expert analyst, Jim Grabowski, and I talked about the game prior to the beginning of the broadcast: what to look for, which LSU players we should be aware of, keys to winning, the topics we should cover in the pregame, that sort of thing. I asked him what his major concern was, and he said, "LSU's speed. They may be too fast for us to cover them." Bingo!

We had to stretch the pregame. The ABC folks decided to delay the start of the game by fifteen minutes. More than 70,000 fans in the Superdome, the players and coaches on both teams, plus the radio and television audiences simply had to wait until TV said it was time to play ball. This was no big surprise. For years, television has run the show. Their gigantic contracts with the NCAA and the various conferences enable them to dictate matchups of teams, when and where games will be played, and at what time. Not to mention the long television commercial breaks, which often extend the length of the game by several minutes. It's a fact of life. We've all gotten used to it.

It was great fun watching and listening to the fans and bands before the game. The Superdome's reputation for being loud is well-deserved.

Illini fans were outnumbered. Estimates were that 20,000 orange and blue faithfuls were matched against 50,000-plus LSU fans. The taunting, cheering, booing, pom-pom waving, and band playing began at least ninety minutes before kickoff and never stopped. It was a terrific collegiate football atmosphere.

At long last, they tossed the coin. Illinois won the toss and elected to defer, thus giving LSU the ball to start the game. We wondered on the broadcast why a team would defer inside a dome, where there was no wind or weather conditions to think about. Obviously, Ron Turner hoped that the Illini could kick off deep, hold them, force a punt, and get the ball in excellent field position. That's exactly what happened, but the Illini weren't able to move the ball any more than the Tigers were.

Then LSU began to roll. As Grabowski had predicted, it was impossible for Illinois to handle the LSU speed. Their quarterback, Rohan Davey, was on target, and his corps of receivers, led by the nation's best pass receiver, Josh Reed, were beating Illini defenders on nearly every pass play. Illinois' vaunted blitz was being picked up, thus giving Davey plenty of time to find his targets.

On the Illinois side, quarterback Kurt Kittner was missing receivers, receivers were dropping passes, passes were being batted down at the line of scrimmage, and the offensive line was giving Kurt very little protection. It was one of the least productive halves that Illinois played all year. When the half was over, LSU led 34-7. For all intents and purposes, the game seemed to be over. Illinois had mounted some great second-half comebacks during the year, but this lead seemed insurmountable, especially against a team that seemed so superior.

The Illini did rally in the second half and showed some of the offensive and defensive skills that had propelled them to a 10-1 season record. But LSU continued to score as well. When it was finally over-and what a long game it was!–LSU had won

47-34. Amazingly, that thirteen-point margin turned out to be the closest of all the BCS games.

During the last quarter of the broadcast, Grabowski turned to me and said, "Since this is your last football broadcast, let's talk about your retirement a little bit."

"I don't think so," I replied. It was the last thing I wanted to do on the air, especially with half of the basketball season remaining to be covered. I wasn't trying to avoid the topic, but I just didn't feel it was appropriate at that time. I still think it was a good call on my part.

During our postgame show, Ron Turner was surprisingly upbeat. He was disappointed with how the team played, especially during the first half. But he said this game would show his team what it is like at the next level and that they had a good chance of making a move toward that level during the 2002 season.

Later, Turner would receive a substantial raise and a contract extension from Illinois to reward him for a fantastic season in 2001 and to keep the wolves from the door; several teams inquired about his availability as the annual coaching carousel spun round and round for several weeks following the end of the season.

Turner said "no" to Stanford and perhaps some others. The season was now over, but what a season it had been. Looking back, it began on a rocky note.

Chapter 3

Preseason

Heading into his fifth season as head coach of the Fighting Illini, Ron Turner thought he had everything and everyone in place to launch into the preseason schedule in early August. But there were at least three stumbling blocks to overcome before practice could begin.

The coach had made some personnel changes. He had to; the Illini defense gave up sixty-one points to Northwestern in the 2000 season finale. Previously against Illinois, Michigan scored thirty-five, Minnesota forty-four, Penn State thirty-nine, Indiana thirty-five, and Ohio State twenty-four. It was obvious that the Illini needed some better defenders and that some defensive coaches had to go. A fresh start was needed.

Turner brought in Mike Cassity from Oklahoma State to be the defensive coordinator and cornerbacks coach. OSU had held national champion Oklahoma to twelve points during the 2000 season, and Cassity's team ranked ninth in the nation in total defense in 1999.

Mike Mallory, a former All-American linebacker and a member of the storied Mallory football coaching family, was hired to coach the safeties. Donnie Thompson, who coached the North Carolina defensive line in 2000, was designated to do the same job for the Illini in 2001.

Three new coaches, all on the defensive side, were an indication that Turner was serious. Turner was confident that the new guys would install an attacking defense to complement the team's solid offensive unit.

Greg Carlson, the long-time head football coach at Wabash College, was hired as Director of Football Operations. Turner was sure that a former head coach would be a natural for DFO, a demanding twenty-four-hour, seven-days-a-week job.

So as Turner and his family took their annual July vacation in Arkansas, everything seemed to be in readiness for the opening of Camp Rantoul and the start of the preseason workouts. But then it hit the fan.

First, Carlson quit. He walked into the football office in late July, turned in his keys and credit cards, and said, "I'm outta here." Although no official reasons are ever given in such personnel matters, it is generally thought that Carlson and Turner didn't get along very well. Carlson, a head coach for such a long time, was used to calling the shots and handing out orders, and he evidently had trouble being on the receiving end. Several people close to the football program reported hearing shouting matches between Turner and Carlson, some of them quite profane.

Turner was able to persuade Doug Green to come back and take over the DFO slot on an interim basis. Green, who came to Illinois with Turner from the Chicago Bears, had resigned to finish law school. With Green in the fold, Turner was able to mark off DFO from his "to-do" list.

The second preseason setback was a shocker. Camp Rantoul would not be available because the groundskeepers had sprayed all the football fields with a chemical that was supposed to fertilize the grass. Instead, all the grass died.

The practice fields turned brown, ugly, and hard as bricks. Turner had no choice but to stay on campus for the preseason. Camp Rantoul was now Camp Champaign. The team would be housed at a local hotel, and the task of keeping everyone together became a little more difficult than it was in isolated Camp Rantoul. There were more distractions (girlfriends, family, etc.) in Champaign.

The third stumbling block was not so much a problem as it was a concern. With the deaths of Minnesota lineman Korey Stringer and Northwestern safety Rashidi Wheeler (occurring within a week of each other during football workouts), national media focus was on all teams working in the heat. Turner and his medical staff were on the spot, as were all coaches and medical staffs, when preseason practice began in early August. Concerns about players' health became big news stories.

Although the autopsy confirmed that Wheeler died of bronchial asthma and not heatstroke, questions still arose regarding the advisability of conducting such physically demanding drills and workouts in the heat and humidity of the Midwest. And Wheeler's death was sparking plenty of questions about asthma and athletes.

The Illini rookies reported on August 5, 2001. On August 6, under sunny skies and hot and humid conditions, they began workouts; on August 8, the full squad reported. The opener at Cal was now less than a month away. With last year's team slumping to 5-6 overall and 2-6 and a ninth-place finish in the Big Ten, it was obvious that this team must do much better, or all the heat that Turner would face wouldn't be just on the football field. At a minimum, his team needed to finish above .500 and get to a bowl game.

Thus the three nonconference games against Cal, Northern Illinois, and Louisville were crucial; the Illini needed to win all three. So as practice began, several difficulties having been overcome, Ron Turner had less than a month to get his team ready for what was already being called a "must-win" game.

Chapter 4

September 11, 2001

It was Monday night, September 10, 2001, and we were having fun on "The Ron Turner Show" at the Alpha Delta Phi fraternity. This call-in radio show that's on fifty stations statewide moves to a different location each week, mostly to fraternity and sorority houses. The young people are always so much fun to be around. They are loud and boisterous and eager to have a good time during their hour with the coach. We take phone calls from the radio audience, those at the house ask questions, we visit with a different Illini player each week, and we play a silly, fun game called "Illini Jeopardy."

On that Monday night, everyone was in a good mood. We talked seriously about football; the upcoming game with the explosive Louisville Cardinals seemed like the most important thing in many of our lives. The students were just getting started on a new semester and were seemingly happy and carefree. They were looking forward to watching Monday Night Football. The next morning, all of our lives would change, perhaps forever.

People always remember where they were when they first heard about horrific happenings. The JFK assassination. Pearl Harbor. FDR's death. Martin Luther King killed. To me, none matched what happened on September 11, 2001.

I get to work around 7:30 a.m. to prepare for my daily talk show, "Penny for Your Thoughts," which is two hours in length. I frequently book interesting guests, but to me the real joy of the show are the open lines, when people can call in on any topic.

To keep abreast of what's happening, I scan *The Champaign-Urbana News-Gazette*, the *Chicago Sun-Times*, the *Chicago Tribune*, and *USA Today*. I also take a quick look at various sites on the Internet.

On that Tuesday morning, I walked into the studio where Stevie Jay was running his morning show and Dave Loane was about halfway through his sportscast. Stevie has a TV set in the studio and usually has it tuned to CNN or Fox. As I entered the studio, Stevie broke in with the news that an airplane had hit one of the towers of the World Trade Center in New York. We were stunned, thinking, "What a terrible accident." We soon learned that it was not a little private plane, but rather a commercial jet. How could an accident like that happen?

Then the second plane hit the other tower. We knew then it was no accident. This was a terrorist attack on the United States of America–on our home turf.

Our staff immediately sprang into action. Everyone who was at work that day and for several days afterward did what they could to gather and dispense information to our audience. We suspended all regular programming, cut out all commercials, and broadcast hour after hour every bit of news we could find from CBS radio, The Associated Press, television, and our own news staff.

The talk show that I had planned for that morning was scrapped, and we began taking calls from listeners. Reaction ranged from shock to rage. "Who did this to us?" they asked, calling for immediate retaliation.

There was no talk of Rep. Gary Condit. No one mentioned Madonna. Not one person said anything about the traffic problem at Green and Prospect. There were no mentions of City Council happenings. Nobody talked about the price of gasoline. The County Board? Nothing. No rumors about basketball recruiting. And not a single word about Saturday's game with Louisville. Suddenly all the things that seemed so big, so important, so controversial, yesterday, were today reduced to small, unimportant, and insignificant. This was an attack on America. Six thousand missing and presumed dead. It was too much to even try to comprehend.

In the wake of this unspeakable act, we carried on at WDWS and WHMS. I was very proud of how everyone performed. It is really what local radio is all about–communicating with local people and helping them when possible.

Later in the week, after the initial shock had subsided a bit, there were decisions to be made regarding the Illinois-Louisville game. Initially, Athletic Director Ron Guenther and Chancellor Nancy Cantor announced that the game would be played. Ron Turner told his team that the game was on, and they cheered. Everyone was looking for an escape from the tragedy, and President Bush had asked us to go forward, to go on with our lives as best we could.

But as it was during the aftermath of the JFK assassination, not everyone was in agreement about what should be done. Some conferences said their games were off, some said they would go ahead.

Later in the week, as more and more conferences postponed games and the entire National Football League schedule was called off, the Big Ten did likewise. The Illinois-Louisville game was pushed back one week.

At 11 a.m. Saturday morning, when the Illinois-Louisville game was to have kicked off, the U of I held a patriotic rally in Memorial Stadium. The Marching Illini were there, along with several singing groups and speakers. At the end of the program, some 8,000 people held hands and sang. It was very emotional and very apparent at that moment that the right decision had been made regarding postponement of the game.

On Monday night, we did another Ron Turner radio show. Coach Turner talked about the difficulty of maintaining the proper focus at practice during that week following the hijackings. But we went on with our lives. We had to because there were no other choices. Even so, things have never felt quite the same. Perhaps the event helped some of us gain some perspective in our lives. Perhaps our priorities had not been in the proper order, and family, faith, and friends moved back to the top of our lists.

September 11, 2001. Dear God, never again.

Chapter 5

Indiana

Sitting in the press box at Memorial Stadium in Bloomington, Indiana, one can get a bad case of vertigo. The same guy must have designed both the football stadium and the basketball arena. If you sit near the top of either one, you feel as if you will fall forward onto the playing field at any moment.

As we sat there waiting for the Illini-Hoosiers game to begin on a dreary and rain-filled October afternoon, I was thinking about one of the strangest sights that I have ever seen on a football field. It happened when Lee Corso was the Indiana coach. Corso, who is now Mr. Smart on ESPN's *Game Day*, thought he was smart back in those days, too. He decided to pull a trick on Illinois and fire up his Hoosiers.

The Illini came out to warm up at the usual time, but there were no Hoosiers on the field. Minutes went by, and people in the stands began to talk to one another:

"Where on earth are the Hoosiers?" The Illini finished their warmups, went back into the locker room for final instructions, and came back out ready to play. Still no Hoosiers. Just the Illinois team and the officials. We joked that Indiana was afraid to show up, but we were all very confused about what was happening.

Then suddenly, the gates at the north end of the stadium swung open and three big double-decker buses rolled onto the field. The Hoosiers, led by Corso, came roaring off the buses onto the field, ready to destroy the Illini. The crowd went crazy. Never before nor since have I seen such a stunt pulled at a college football game. It was pure theater! It was pure Corso!

Oh, by the way, Illinois won big. Corso's Hoosiers weren't very good, and soon the Showman was on his way out the door. Obviously, he belongs on television and not on the playing field. He is a lot smarter on TV.

Cam Cameron's 2001 Hoosiers had stunned the football world the week before playing the Illini by rolling up sixty-three points and destroying Wisconsin in Madison. Antwaan Randle El and tailback Levron Williams played sensational games, and the victory no doubt preserved Cameron's job, at least for the time being.

But our game turned out to be all Illinois as Ron Turner's team won its fifth game of the season, pounding the Hoosiers 35-14. Kurt Kittner threw only seventeen passes, and the Illini rediscovered their ground game. But the real story of the game was the defense played by Mike Cassity's guys. They contained Randle El and allowed just two touchdowns. With each passing week, it was becoming more and more apparent that the success of Illinois was dependent upon the attacking, gambling defensive unit.

The drive home from Bloomington after the game was terrible. A monsoon-type rainstorm covered the area, and it was close to four hours of white-knuckling the steering wheel. But there was joy in knowing that the Illini were just one victory from becoming bowl-eligible with Wisconsin coming to town for Illinois' homecoming game the following Saturday.

It would be my last trip to Memorial Stadium in Bloomington, and I found it a little more than ironic that one of my lasting memories of the place was of Lee Corso's double-decker buses. I wonder if they have ever discussed that on *Game Day*?

Chapter 6

Wisconsin

There are days in autumn in the Midwest when the conditions are just right for college football. The leaves are turning into brilliant colors, the sun is bright, and there is a comfortable, almost soothing chill in the air. The oppressive heat from summer is gone, and the bone-chilling winter weather is close by but has not yet arrived.

From the press box at Memorial Stadium, one can see for miles. Up close are the tailgaters, some of whom have arrived the night before. The magnificent U of I campus, built by thoughtful people who decided long ago that all buildings should look like they belong together, is impressive. Beyond the buildings are the black-dirt farmlands of Champaign County.

October 20, 2001 was such a day, and the Wisconsin Badgers were in town. Eventually, more than 70,000 fans, a rare sellout at Memorial Stadium, would make their way to the venue. They drove, biked, bused, and walked from all directions. I watched all of this and suddenly became a bit teary-eyed, knowing that there wouldn't be many more days when I would be a part of the action as play-by-play man for the Fighting Illini. Just two more home games–Penn State and Northwestern.

Wisconsin had won nine of its last ten and twelve of its last fourteen road games, and Illinois had not beaten the Badgers the last six times the teams had played. The two schools had not met since a 37-3 Badger win in Champaign in 1998. I have nightmares about Ron Dayne running over our over-matched Illini time and again.

Two of the most memorable Illini-Badger matchups took place in Madison. I did the play-by-play for one; in the other, I wore a tuxedo and listened to the game in the parking lot of Westminster Church in Springfield.

The first was in 1959, as the Ray Eliot era was coming to an end. The legendary Illini coach, famous for his fiery speeches and upsets at homecoming games, was struggling with his last team. Going into the Wisconsin game, the Illini had won three, lost three and tied one. Ray's last team was led by Bill Burrell, a linebacker who finished fourth in the Heisman trophy balloting and was named the most valuable player in the Big Ten by the *Chicago Tribune*.

But it was fullback Bill Brown who provided the heroics on that day, plunging over for a touchdown as time on the clock expired, giving Iliinois a hard-fought 9-6 victory. The following Saturday, the Illini beat Northwestern 28-0 in Memorial Stadium to wind up the season 5-3-1. Brown rushed for 164 yards, and Burrell's defensive unit permitted Northwestern to go past midfield just once all afternoon.

In 1982, the Illini and Badgers played a game in Madison that had one of the most thrilling finishes in Illinois football history. The date was October 23, the same day that my daughter, Christine, got married in Springfield. As the see-saw game wound down, the church was beginning to fill up and the photographer was calling me to get over there with the rest of the wedding party to take some photographs. But I couldn't leave the radio and Rick Atterberry, who was filling in for me on the play-by-play.

I couldn't believe it when the Wisconsin quarterback threw a bounce-pass lateral off the turf to receiver Al Toon, who promptly threw a touchdown pass. I almost shut the radio off at that point, but I'm sure glad I didn't. The Illini came back with a long gainer on a pass from Tony Eason to Tim Brewster. Mike Bass then hurried onto the field and kicked the game-winning field goal in the final seconds. Illinois won 29-28. I hurried to walk my daughter down the aisle, and it was a wonderful day.

The 2001 game in Champaign was almost as dramatic. The Illini jumped out to a big lead, much to the delight of the homecoming crowd. Illinois opened the scoring with a field goal by Peter Christofilakos, but Wisconsin came back with a quick touchdown to make it 7-3 Badgers. Then Illinois scored two more field goals and two touchdowns to take a 23-7 lead at halftime. A third-quarter field goal gave Illinois a 26-7 lead. Illini fans were settling back and enjoying the rout. But Wisconsin, taking advantage of Illini turnovers, rallied and took the lead, 35-28, in the fourth quarter.

Ron Turner's crew came roaring back as quarterback Kurt Kittner hit tight end Brian Hodges with a fourteen-yard touchdown pass to tie it 35-35. The Illini defense forced a Wisconsin punt, and Illinois marched down the field, scoring the winning touchdown on a pass from Kittner to Brandon Lloyd. Lloyd barely got one foot down as he went out of bounds in the end zone. It was 42-35 Illinois, but there was still enough time remaining for Wisconsin to come back. The Illini held once again, Wisconsin punted, and the Illini were able to run out the clock. It was a rare home win over a very good team. Previously, most of Illinois' big wins under Ron Turner had come on the road.

Illinois went 6-1 with a bye week before tackling the hardest part of the schedule: Purdue and Ohio State on the road and Penn State and Northwestern at home. Being bowl-eligible on October 21 was a very good feeling.

Chapter 7

Penn State

I have always listed the 1994 Illinois-Penn State game in Memorial Stadium as one of the most thrilling broadcasts of my career. Some find this quite peculiar, since Penn State won that game 35-31. No Illini fan will ever forget that last-ditch drive of more than ninety yards directed by Penn State quarterback Kerry Collins, with Brian Milne rumbling in for the winning touchdown in the final seconds of the game. At Penn State they still refer to "The Drive." When the game broadcast was over, I was mentally and physically drained, as was anyone who watched it. But I can remember thinking we had just witnessed a wonderful example of collegiate football at its best. I was proud to have been there and to have been a small part of it. It was truly unforgettable.

Penn State continued to dominate the Illini, winning nine of ten games in the series leading up to the November 10, 2001, matchup in Champaign. Penn State opened the season by losing its first four games to Miami, Michigan, Wisconsin, and Iowa. The support for legendary coach Joe Paterno was dwindling, and there was little joy in Happy Valley. But suddenly, Joe Pa inserted a freshman quarterback named Zack Mills into the lineup. The Nittany Lions won three straight and were extremely confident when they rolled into town to face the Illini before a sellout crowd of 70,904.

Little did we realize when Penn State kicked off to the Illini on another sun-drenched, glorious fall afternoon, that we were about to see another truly unforgettable game, a game that would see another long drive in the waning minutes and another winning touchdown. But this time that quarterback was named Kurt Kittner, the running back who scored the big TD was named Rocky Harvey, and the winning team was named Illinois. This time the final score was 33-28.

Again, we were all drained–mentally and physically. In many ways, the victory was a satisfying payback for the 1994 loss. From now on, when people talk about the 1994 game, they will be obligated to include the 2001 game in their conversation.

The only downer on this November afternoon was a broken wrist suffered by Illinois' powerful running back Antoineo Harris. The word after the game was that he would miss the remaining two games against Ohio State and Northwestern, and perhaps the bowl game as well. With Harris sidelined, Rocky Harvey and Carey Davis would share the running back duties with help from freshman Cory Flisakowski. None of those players had the brute strength and "run-over-them" ability of Harris, so it was a major concern for Ron Turner.

With the victory over Penn State, the Illini moved to 8-1 overall, 5-1 in the Big Ten conference and tied for first place with Michigan. The comeback victories were so entertaining and exciting that one wondered what could possibly happen next.

Consider these statistics:

1. The Illini trailed Northern Illinois 6-3 in the fourth quarter before scoring two touchdowns to win.

2. They held a shaky 7-6 lead over Minnesota late in the third quarter, then exploded to win 35-14.

3. They trailed Wisconsin 35-28 in the fourth quarter, and then won on two Kurt Kittner touchdown passes.

4. They fell behind Purdue 13-0, then scored 38 unanswered points to win 38-13.

5. They trailed Penn State 21-7, then took a 27-21 lead. They fell back 28-27, and then won it 33-28.

Whew!

Chapter 8

Northwestern

Thanksgiving Day arrived much the same as other days during the 2001 football season–unseasonably warm and dry. Seldom has a football season gone by without at least one rain or snowstorm, freezing temperatures, and icy winds. Heavy parkas, boots, and mittens were, for the most part, left home as Ron Turner and his Illini continued their magical march toward a Big Ten championship and a major bowl bid. The weather worked in Turner's favor, with his heavy reliance on the passing of Kurt Kittner to any one of a number of swift receivers.

But Thanksgiving Day 2001 was special to me for two reasons: first and foremost, a victory today over Northwestern would mean at least a share of the Big Ten title for the first time since 1990. An Illinois victory today, combined with an Ohio State upset over Michigan in Ann Arbor the following Saturday would mean an undisputed championship–the first for the Illini since 1983, when Mike White's team beat every other Big Ten team on the way to the Rose Bowl.

Second, this would be my final broadcast in Memorial Stadium.

My routine that day didn't change very much, except I found myself more aware of what was going on around me, perhaps hoping to hold onto it a bit longer, perhaps to store it away forever.

Louise rode with me to the stadium; she wanted to be there early to greet friends and relatives who were to gather at the WDWS/WHMS tent before kickoff. We pulled into the northwest Assembly Hall parking lot, and I parked in my favorite spot, right up against a tall light pole so I could find my car when the game was over. There's nothing sorrier than seeing an old geezer wandering through the lot trying to remember where he parked.

Louise and I walked together to the tent, where radio station colleagues, clients, friends, and others were beginning to gather for our traditional pregame meal. After greeting many of them, I began a slow walk toward the press gate on the west side of Memorial Stadium. So many times I had made this trek, never once speaking to anyone, just staring straight ahead, anxious to get to the radio booth and begin preparations for the broadcast. But this time it was different. People recognized me, shouted, "Hey, Turp, we gonna get these guys today?" I smiled and said I sure hoped so. Many were cooking out. Some had prepared elaborate Thanksgiving Day dinners to be eaten in or beside their RVs or tents. Most were clad in orange and blue. I noticed, for the first time, how elaborate some of the sweaters and sweatshirts were. How many kooky hats and vests and gloves people were wearing. Some were throwing a football. One man was leading a little boy by the hand; the kid was just learning to walk, but he had on an orange sweat suit, never too young to get that Illini spirit going.

As I walked toward the press gate, I began thinking about the last time the Illini had played a game on Thanksgiving Day. It was 1963 in East Lansing, Michigan.

Following the assassination of President John F. Kennedy, many games were postponed, but the Illinois/Michigan State game was still scheduled, until Saturday morning. The team had flown to East Lansing, gone through all the pregame preparations, and was ready to go play when word came that the game had been postponed until the following Thursday–Thanksgiving Day.

The Spartans were ranked No. 4 in the nation, and their roster was filled with All-Americans and future NFL players. Sherm Lewis was considered one of the best running backs in the nation. But the Illini, led by Dick Butkus and Jim Grabowski, were up to the challenge. When it was all over, Illinois had forced three MSU fumbles and picked off four interceptions, winning 13-0. On that day Illinois won the Big Ten championship and got a trip to the Rose Bowl. Would this Thanksgiving Day be as productive?

(One side note on the 1963 game: MSU Coach Duffy Daugherty swore for years that had the game been played on Saturday and not postponed until the following Thursday, his Spartans would have won. "We were ready on Saturday, but not on Thursday," the affable Spartans coach contended. I told Dick Butkus that story one day, and he just laughed. "We would have beaten those @#$!#@$$ Spartans on any day of the week!" I would never doubt Mr. Butkus.)

As I entered the press gate and waited for the elevator, I exchanged greetings with several members of the media, many of them long-time friends. If any of them realized that this was to be my last broadcast from Memorial Stadium, none said so. We talked instead about Illini-Northwestern games from the past. How many times did the Wildcats, long before they became Big Ten contenders, upset the Illini on the final game of the season? It was too painful to think about. All we had to do today was beat Northwestern, and we would at least tie for the Big Ten championship. But the memories of those previous-game upsets would stay in the backs of our minds. "At least it won't be 0-0," predicted one wag.

Illinois and Northwestern played to a 0-0 tie in 1978 that must rank as one of the most futile afternoons ever, not only for the football teams involved, but also for the radio announcing team. What can you say? How can you make a game like that sound exciting? About the best thing you can say about it is that it was close! If a tie game is "like kissing your sister," what on earth is a 0-0 tie like? I remember leaving the press box that day totally depressed.

Later that same year, Illinois and Wisconsin played to a 20-20 tie as part of Gary Moeller's second year as head coach; the Illini finished 1-8-2. Moeller's first Illinois team in 1977 had gone 3-8-0. His third and final team was 2-8-1. Moeller's three-year record was 6-24-3. Small wonder that he was fired and replaced by Mike White prior to the 1980 season.

But I wasn't thinking of Gary Moeller or Mike White as I left the elevator and headed for the broadcast booth. I was thinking that it would never be like this again for me. I already had my strategy planned; I was not going to mention this as my final broadcast in Memorial Stadium on the air. I hoped that none of my broadcast partners (Jim Grabowski, Brian Barnhart, and Brooks Parriott) would mention it either. I wanted only to do the game to the best of my ability and sign off, as usual, "I'm Jim Turpin; goodbye for now." Illinois was certain to play in a bowl game, so I would have one more broadcast to do anyway, but no matter how important the bowl game, I knew it would not be the same as my last broadcast in Memorial Stadium.

The photo deck level in the press box is where the food is served, so that is the natural gathering place for the media. Free food means many media, no matter the venue. The food this day was outstanding, a traditional Thanksgiving dinner with all the trimmings. As usual, I ate nothing. I have never been able to eat right before a broadcast. Burping on the air is bad manners and a bit unprofessional.

After exchanging a few barbs and quips with some long-time media friends, I went directly to our broadcast booth, which is on the same level as the photo deck. Our engineer, Ed Bond, had everything set up and ready to go for the broadcast and had gone out for lunch. None of the other members of the broadcast team were there yet, so I was alone. I proceeded to set up my flip charts, tape my notes to the table, focus my field glasses and set them down, and begin to concentrate on Illinois-Northwestern 2001. But it just didn't work. My mind drifted:

• 1956–Looking onto the Memorial Stadium turf, I can still see Abe Woodson running seventy yards for one touchdown and going eighty-two yards for another TD on a screen pass from Bill Offenbecher as Illinois upset Michigan State, the nation's No. 1 team, 20-13. The year before, Illinois had upset Michigan 25-6 when the Wolverines were No. 1 in the nation.

• 1956–I worked that Illinois/MSU game with Harry Caray. He was the play-by-play man, and I was his spotter. Harry worked the game standing up. He tromped on everyone's feet, including mine, as he rattled around the booth describing a game that he would later say was the most exciting he had ever called. Considering all the great, exciting St. Louis Cardinal baseball games he had called, that was quite a statement.

• 1951–I was a senior at Olney High School when I saw my first Illinois game. It was against Michigan and was played in a driving snowstorm. Illini quarterback Tommy

O'Connell hit end Rex Smith with a short touchdown pass in the final minutes, and Illinois won 7-0 on the way to a 9-0-1 season which included a 40-7 thrashing of Stanford in the 1952 Rose Bowl. Players from both teams held a fiftieth-year reunion of that game during the 2002 Rose Bowl festivities in Pasadena.

• 1983–As I looked to the eastern sideline, there was Thomas Rooks making one of the most memorable touchdown runs ever to close out a 17-13 win over Ohio State, as Mike White's team became the first Big Ten team in history to beat all nine conference opponents. Down 13-10, Illinois made a fantastic drive that was spearheaded by the passing of Jack Trudeau and the receiving of Scott Golden. They were hoping to get in position for a game-tying field goal, and that's when Rooks made his touchdown dash. No Illini will ever forget that moment.

• There was Ray Eliot in that brown topcoat and hat, stalking the sideline. Across the field was Woody Hayes of Ohio State in his short sleeves and baseball cap. The battle had begun! What fun!

• 1980–There was Dave Wilson, Mike White's first quarterback, throwing a long incomplete pass on the first play of the game and drawing a standing ovation from the Illini fans. Obviously, the Gary Moeller era was over, and the White era had begun.

• Who can ever forget the many times Chief Illiniwek has done his halftime dance? Chills and thrills each and every time for true Illini fans and friends. You can read my thoughts on the Chief controversy in chapter 41, but as I sat there on that Thanksgiving morning, I must say that the Chief was right there with the football memories.

• 1963–Dick Butkus lumbered onto the field to anchor a superb Illinois defense. An award is given every year to the nation's best collegiate linebacker; it is called the Butkus Award. That's how good he was. And I could picture my broadcast partner for so many years, Jim Grabowski (a Hall-of-Famer himself), running over people and establishing himself as one of Illinois' greatest ball carriers.

• There are the quarterbacks: Dave Wilson, Tony Eason, Jack Trudeau, Jeff George, Jason Verduzco, Johnny Johnson, and now Kurt Kittner. What a thrill for a play-by-play announcer to describe their passing heroics!

The door to the broadcast booth opened; it was Ed, back from lunch. It was time for him to start talking to the network stations. My flashbacks were over for now. And a good thing, too. Time to start thinking about today's game with Northwestern and a possible Big Ten championship.

As time went on, Grabowski arrived and began going over the research material that he prepared in advance. Athletic Director Ron Guenther popped in, chatted with Grabowski, and wished us all a good broadcast. (He often returns several times during the game. I don't know where he hangs out, but I know he moves from his private booth to the broadcast booth to the top of the press box with the cops, and who knows where else.) There was a lot at stake that day, and Ron was nervous. Everyone was. Illinois was a big favorite, but that means little when Northwestern comes to town.

Finally it was time for the broadcast to begin. Grabowski, Parriott, and I did a brief intro, then turned it over to Barnhart for the rest of the pregame, including an interview with Coach Ron Turner and several Illini players. Just prior to kickoff, Barnhart turned the broadcast back to us, and my last call in Memorial Stadium began.

It was a typical Illinois-Northwestern struggle, with the lead going back and forth, and the outcome was very much in doubt until the final minutes. The Illini eventually won it 34-28. The postgame was terrific, with highlights of the victory, a good interview with a joyous Ron Turner, and a lot of good feelings in the broadcast booth after a 10-1 season. Remember, we had been through a 0-11 season, too. Trust me, 10-1 is a lot more fun! After Barnhart wrapped up the statistics, I thanked the network stations and our sponsors and told them we would be in touch about the bowl game. As planned, I signed off, "I'm Jim Turpin, good-bye for now."

Then I gathered up my stuff, thanked Jim, Brian, Brooks, and Ed for a superb broadcast, and headed out the broadcast booth door. I wasn't quite prepared for what happened next.

Outside the door were my wife, my children, and my grandchildren. They had somehow talked their way up the press elevator. They wanted to be there when I walked out of that broadcast booth for the last time. It touched me deeply. We hugged and kissed and cried. I will never forget that moment.

We took photographs of each other, took some shots of the now empty stadium, and some shots of the campus buildings in the distance. As I think back, it was as if we all knew this would be our last time together in the press box and we wanted to hold on to this special moment. As we continued to talk and snap photographs, my daughter Chris asked me to sit down for one last shot. She wanted to get me, the stadium, and the Assembly Hall all in one shot. The photograph appears on the cover of this book. Then, the last ride down the elevator as Illinois' play-by-play announcer. It was so comforting to have the family with me. It was a tough day for this old man.

Section 2

THE
COACHES

Chapter 9

Lou Tepper

When Lou Tepper was named head football coach at the U of I in December 1991 his opening statement at the press conference was:

"The three most important things in my life are my faith, my family, and my football team."

A cynical member of the press sitting behind me muttered, "If he doesn't win some games, he may have to change his priorities."

Tepper, lauded in an ESPN special on race relations, eventually would lose his job because he didn't win enough games. I doubt that he changed his priorities.

Tepper's downfall came very quickly and was brought on by a decision he made regarding assistant coach Greg Landry. Landry, a former NFL quarterback, was Illinois' offensive coordinator. Tepper's team, with quarterback Johnny Johnson throwing four touchdown passes, was coming off a 30-0 win over East Carolina in the 1994 Liberty Bowl. With many players returning, Illini football fortunes were looking up. In addition, Landry had just recruited Chris Redmon from Louisville, Kentucky, who was one of the nation's most highly rated quarterbacks.

Tepper never made public his reasons for firing Landry, but the rumors were that Landry, while in Louisville recruiting Redmon for Illinois, had made a pitch to become head coach at the University of Louisville. Landry denied it, but Tepper went ahead with the firing. The Redmon family was incensed, because the chief reason that Chris was coming to Illinois was Landry. The Redmons drove to Champaign to meet with Tepper and demanded that Chris be released from his commitment to Illinois. Tepper quickly granted the release. Chris wound up staying at home and setting every passing record in the history of University of Louisville football.

Tepper hired his long-time friend Paul Schudel, who was head coach at Ball State at the time, to become Illinois' offensive coordinator, replacing Landry.

It didn't work. The Illini were pathetic on offense under Schudel. Tepper's two bad decisions ultimately cost him his job in 1996.

I liked Lou Tepper. He was and is a man of faith and integrity. I can't say that about all the coaches I have met during my thirty years of broadcasting. I hope Lou and his family are very happy.

Chapter 10

Harv Schmidt

We were sitting at an outdoor restaurant in Miami, sipping a drink and having a sandwich. It was late at night on December 28, 1968 perhaps, the happiest night in Harv Schmidt's seven-year tenure as the head basketball coach at the University of Illinois. Illinois had just won the Hurricane Classic and was undefeated.

"Do you believe this? Can you believe that we're 10-0 and sitting outside three days after Christmas, having a beer? Better enjoy it tonight, guys, it doesn't get much better than this," said the former Kankakee and Illinois star who had led his alma mater back to basketball respectability. Schmidt had been an assistant coach at New Mexico for three years when he was picked in 1967 to lead the Illini, following the resignation of Harry Combes in the wake of the slush fund scandal.

Combes's last team (1966-67) finished 12-12 overall and 6-8 in the Big Ten conference. Combes, his assistant Howie Braun, and head football coach Pete Elliott all lost their jobs following Illinois' most infamous sports scandal.

Schmidt, with no head coaching experience, was quickly brought in to right a sinking ship. His first team was 11-13 overall and 6-8 in the conference. On December 2, 1967, the Illini won 75-57 at Butler; it was Schmidt's first game as head coach.

"Well, there's no way we can lose 'em all now," the new coach quipped after the game. It brought a smile to the faces of Illini reporters and broadcasters who had suffered through the slush fund scandal. Here was a bright, young, energetic former Illini player who immediately gave us all hope that things would be better.

Schmidt's career at Illinois soared during his first few years. The Illini led the nation in attendance in 1970, and every pre-tipoff appearance by Schmidt at the Assembly Hall was greeted with a standing ovation. As he lumbered up the tunnel ramp, the cheering began, and it would continue for minutes. Outside, a light shined from the Assembly Hall to a Memorial Stadium wall where a giant "I Like Harv" sign was displayed. I have never witnessed such an ovation for a coach before or after Schmidt.

I don't think there has ever been a more popular coach at Illinois than Schmidt during his early years. Sadly, his career at Illinois ended with his firing in 1974. Schmidt was so bitter about it that he hasn't seen an Illini game or returned to the campus since he was let go.

Schmidt's 1968-69 team was one of my all-time favorites. I loved every player on that team and my affection for Schmidt made it all that much more enjoyable.

Included in that opening 10-0 run was a 97-84 win at Houston, which broke the Cougars' sixty-game home winning streak. Houston had beaten the Illini the year before on the way to a 31-2 record.

The Illini were captained by Dave Scholz, a rugged 6'8" forward from Decatur. The other forward was Fred Miller. Greg Jackson was the center and Jodie Harrison and Mike Price were the starting guards. Each of them had a distinct and enduring personality, and each made significant contributions as the team rolled to a 19-5 overall record. Their 9-5 Big Ten mark was good enough for a second-place tie, and the final AP poll ranked Illinois twentieth in the nation. It was a remarkable turnaround from just two years prior.

Many other Illini teams have done better; there have been better records, higher finishes in the league, higher national rankings. But there was something about this particular team that made Illini fans happy and proud. Mostly I think it was the way they gutted out victories they had no business winning. Schmidt loved to talk about the way Scholz would "stick out his chin and simply will victories. He just wouldn't let us get beaten." It was a team to love. But despite this promising start and the overwhelming popularity of the coach and the players, Schmidt never had another Illinois team that finished in the top twenty-five.

Schmidt's team the following year (1969-70) went 15-9 and 8-6 in the conference as Randy Crews and Rick Howat joined Price, Miller, and Jackson in the starting lineup. They finished a respectable third in the Big Ten.

The one criticism that many had of Schmidt was that he failed to recruit highly regarded black players. Mike Price was ultimately a first-round NBA draft choice, and Greg Jackson was a respectable center, but there was a general feeling that Schmidt couldn't take Illinois to a higher level without bigger and better black players. So he set out to find some.

First came two players from Ohio, Nick Weatherspoon (Canton) and Nick Connor (Columbus). Both lettered in 1971, 1972, and 1973. Weatherspoon was a thin, wiry, strong scoring machine who set several Illini records. The NBA's Washington Bullets drafted "Spoon" in the first round. He, too, was a popular player among the Illini faithful.

But two other players recruited at about that same time (Billy Morris from St. Louis and Alvin O'Neal from Peoria) weren't as successful as Spoon and were seemingly in trouble most of the time with Schmidt and the university. Schmidt did his best to balance the need for their presence on the court with the need to maintain discipline, but it was a losing battle. I recall one time when Morris just didn't show up for a plane trip to Michigan State. It was unclear as to whether he had overslept or simply decided to pass on this particular game.

The problem exploded when the team captain, Jim Krelle from Aurora West, quit the team, maintained that Schmidt was guilty of having two sets of standards for his players.

Krelle said one set of standards applied to white players and a different set of standards applied to black players. It was an ugly accusation, and it was not something that Schmidt needed with his now-struggling program.

The 1973-74 team was Schmidt's last. It won just five games and lost eighteen. The Big Ten conference mark was 2-12. The Illini finished tenth in the Big Ten. It was rock bottom. The seven-year Schmidt roller-coaster ride was over.

No one took defeat worse than Schmidt. His postgame television appearances after losses were very painful to watch. He would often spend the entire interview staring at the floor, never looking at the camera.

On the road after a defeat, Schmidt would say, "Turp, you want to have a cup of coffee?" I always wanted to. I always tried to show compassion and to comfort him in any possible way. The cup of coffee often turned into several cups of coffee and an all-night conversation in some diner somewhere, trying to figure out what went wrong. Despite the reason we were there, and disregarding the atmosphere in those greasy, late-night joints, I remember with great fondness when it was just the two of us talking basketball.

So it was no surprise that Schmidt took his dismissal hard. Years later when another Illini team was playing in Denver (where Schmidt lived), Loren Tate and I had lunch with Harv, and we had a great time. We told stories and laughed and remembered the good times. We gave Harv tickets for the game that night, but he never showed. He let his son use the tickets. Apparently he still can't bear to watch the orange and blue. It must bring back too many bad memories for him.

The Illini hired Gene Bartow to replace Schmidt. He lasted one year. His 1974-75 team, captained by Rick Schmidt, went 8-18 overall and 4-14 in the conference. The Illini finished ninth in the conference standings.

After that first year, Bartow was hired away by UCLA to replace John Wooden. Next was Lou Henson, who coached the Illini for twenty-one years and restored the program to national prominence.

Chapter 11

Lou Henson

L ou Henson called a meeting one hot afternoon in the summer of 2001. "Be there at 3 p.m.," he told us. The meeting time fit between the luncheon Lou had with a few of us and the dinner party he and his wife Mary were hosting that night. Lou had been up at 5 a.m., walked his three miles, played nine holes of golf, and attended two business meetings. He was sixty-nine years old at the time.

We were a little surprised that the 3 p.m. meeting Lou put together was at Hooters! It started with six or seven friends, then grew to twenty, including current Illini coach Bill Self and one of his assistants, Billy Gillespie. I don't recall being at a get-together where there were more stories, more laughs or more fun; it was a joy to be there. About 5 p.m., Lou said he had to go home and help Mary fix dinner (not likely). He picked up the tab for the group and hustled away. The man has some energy! He and Mary spend some time in Champaign during the summer before returning to Las Cruces for another season with New Mexico State. He makes the most of every minute in Champaign. He is amazing!

During most of the time I spent broadcasting Illini games, Lou Henson was the basketball coach. I consider him a very good friend. But the Henson years at Illinois were like a roller-coaster ride. There were some unbelievably wonderful times and some down times that were both sad and hurtful.

On April 5, 1975, Illinois Athletic Director Cecil Coleman stunned everyone when he picked Henson to succeed Gene Bartow. Bartow had spent just one season at Illinois before departing for UCLA. Henson's hiring prompted headlines which read "LOU WHO?" Not much was known in the Midwest about this 43-year-old coach from New Mexico State. Media speculation centered on Virginia Tech's Don DeVoe, Kansas State's Jack Hartman, and two of Bartow's assistants, Tony Yates and LeRoy Hunt.

Henson's first team at Illinois (1975-76) won its first five games, but finished the season 14-13. The breakthrough year was the 1978-79 season, when the Illini started out 15-0 and had a thrilling win over Magic Johnson and Michigan State. Henson's team made it to the semifinals of the NIT in 1979-80, and then in 1980-81 they qualified for the NCAA tournament for the first time in eighteen years.

Henson's best team was the 1989 Final Four qualifier, led by Nick Anderson, Kendall Gill, Lowell Hamilton, Steve Bardo, and Kenny Battle. That team wound up 31-5 with a loss to Michigan in the NCAA semifinals. The Illini had beaten Michigan with ease in both Champaign and Ann Arbor before meeting the Wolverines for the third time in Seattle. Henson had previously taken New Mexico State to the Final Four, becoming just the ninth coach to pilot two teams to the promised land.

Henson's team had eleven seasons of twenty victories or more. He was named Big Ten Coach of the Year in 1993.

Despite his piling up victory after victory, Henson's critics never let up. Late in his career they began to say he was too old; the game had passed him by; he couldn't relate to young players; he couldn't recruit, Jimmy Collins was doing most of the recruiting anyhow, they said. As more and more people, especially Illini money-backers from Chicago, said it was time for Lou to go, AD Ron Guenther listened.

On road trips, Lou, Loren Tate, and I would have long conversations about what Lou should do. Should he resign? If so, when and how? Should he just stay on and force Guenther's hand? What about Jimmy Collins? Would he be given a chance to succeed Henson? What about Henson's other long-time assistants, Dick Nagy and Mark Coomes? What would be in their future?

My advice to Henson was to make the first move. If he was going to be asked to resign, and it certainly seemed that was what was going to happen, why not go out on his own terms? Make his own announcement. Hold his own press conference. And do it while the season was still going on. I wanted to make sure that the fans had a chance to pay tribute to Lou at the end of the season after the final game in the Assembly Hall. If he waited until the season was over and made the announcement, chances are that any tribute to him wouldn't draw 16,000-plus fans as the final game would. He deserved the big crowd; it just seemed the right thing to do.

Lou agreed that he would make the announcement on his postgame radio show, which I hosted and which was heard on fifty stations statewide. Then he would go down to the interview room and answer questions from the press. It sounded like a good plan to me.

So after the Iowa game, Lou did just that. He read from a statement that he and Mary had prepared. It was very emotional. Fans gathered around the broadcast area to hear the postgame after every Illini game; this time they were shocked at what they heard. They began to shout, "No, no, no." But Lou proceeded to read his statement.

When he was finished, I began to ask him questions, such as "Lou, why did you decide to do this at this time?" In typical Henson fashion, he insisted that the decision to step down was his alone. He was not pressured to do so. He wanted to spend more time with his family. He had coached long enough. Lou Henson was and is too classy to tell the truth about the difficult situation that had developed. To this day, I have never heard him criticize anyone at Illinois–not Ron Guenther, not anyone–for the way it all happened.

He had plenty of reasons to be hurt. For his entire tenure at Illinois, he operated under impossible circumstances. He had no place to practice. His team never knew from one day to the next whether they were going to practice at the Intramural Physical Education building, Kenney Gym, Parkland College, or at some high school, because the Assembly Hall was in use for monster trucks or Garth Brooks or the Ice Capades. Lou's office space was a joke: a desk, a conference table, tapes piled upon tapes; Collins' office was the size of a broom closet. When recruits came in, the coaches tried to show them other things. Under these circumstances, Henson and his staff recruited well and won a bunch of games. Little appreciation was shown.

There was a very nice tribute after the final game of the season against Minnesota. All 16,000 fans stayed around to applaud and cheer as the governor, the president of the university, members of the Board of Trustees, the athletic director, and others sang Henson's praises. They gave him a lot of gifts, including a golf cart. I had the pleasure of being the MC for the event, and I do think many people were sincere in what they said about the departing coach. However, I had this lingering thought when Lou and Mary walked off the Assembly Hall floor, arm in arm, "Well, the Henson detractors got what they wanted. There will be a new, young coach, and Henson will be a good company man and fade off into the sunset." He deserved better, in my opinion.

What a thrill it was to learn later that Lou was hired to coach again at New Mexico State. A new start, a new life, among people who loved and respected what the coach had done for their town, their university, and their state. Lou Henson has always been an ambassador of good will; in New Mexico he is a legend. And he is appreciated.

After Lou's resignation announcement, speculation immediately began regarding who the next coach would be. One coach it wouldn't be was Jimmy Collins. Collins indicated that Guenther had promised him a shot at the job, but Guenther announced that the coach he was looking for would have to have met certain criteria–successful head coaching experience and a trip to the Final Four being two of them. Collins was and is very bitter about the whole situation, feeling that he was never considered even though Guenther had indicated he would be.

Any conversation on that topic between Collins and Guenther is not known to me; I'm only repeating what has been written in the press and what I learned in private conversations with others.

Collins was eventually named head coach at Illinois-Chicago and was able to take Nagy, Coomes, Gene Cross, and Andrew Haring with him. Long-time Illinois-Chicago coach Bob Hallberg wound up odd man out when Collins took his place.

Collins and his staff have done well at Illinois-Chicago. Nagy has resigned from the staff and now handles color commentary on the Flames' radio network. Cross has moved across town to become an assistant coach at DePaul. Following this past season, Collins was rewarded with a contract extension. Time heals all wounds, someone once said. But not always completely.

Chapter 12

Bruce Pearl

Recruiting of high school or junior college athletes can be nasty.

Remember Bruce Pearl?

No Illini fan can forget, and most can never forgive, what the former University of Iowa assistant coach did to the Illinois basketball program and to Jimmy Collins, who was Lou Henson's top assistant and recruiter.

Illinois and Iowa were both recruiting Deon Thomas, a sensational high school player from Chicago's Simeon High School. Pearl and Collins were the point men in this recruiting battle some fourteen years ago. Collins is now the head coach at University of Illinois-Chicago and Pearl is the head coach at University of Wisconsin-Milwaukee.

After repeated long distance calls from Pearl to Thomas, in which Pearl tried time and time again to get Thomas to say that he was being offered illegal inducements by Collins and the Illini, Thomas finally said, "Uh-huh, yeah, right." Pearl had asked whether Illinois had offered Thomas $80,000 and a new Chevy Blazer. Thomas said later that he said "yes" just to get Pearl off his back and stop the late-night phone calls from Iowa City.

Thomas never knew that all his phone conversations with Pearl were being tape-recorded! After getting Thomas to say "yes," Pearl turned the tape over to the NCAA.

After a long investigation, the NCAA couldn't prove any of the charges against Collins, Henson and Illinois. Illinois was ultimately charged with "lack of institutional control" and an NCAA staffer made one of the most ludicrous statements I've ever heard. He said, "Just because we couldn't prove it, doesn't mean they aren't guilty." Thomas's attorney, J. Steven Beckett, said, "In the court system we have a name for that: it's called 'innocent'."

Ironically, Beckett uncovered a number of apparent violations of NCAA rules by Pearl during the recruitment of Thomas, including gifts of cash to buy a jogging suit, meals, transportation, and a number of other extra benefits for Thomas's friends and family. The NCAA never investigated any of these apparent violations, although Beckett turned all of his findings over to them.

Collins hasn't forgotten.

As reported by Loren Tate in a column printed in the January 19, 2002 *Champaign-Urbana News-Gazette*, Collins said, "Pearl dragged me, the University, and our team through the mud. I couldn't respond back then because of a gag order. This time, I'm not going to take it. I just talked to Deon (Thomas) this week, and he said he would be willing to fly back from Spain to testify on all the illegal offers Pearl made."

Collins refused to shake hands with Pearl when their two teams met in early January. Collins sent word to Pearl before the game to "just play the game and stay on your end of the court." Pearl made a big deal about trying to shake Jimmy's hand, but it just wasn't going to happen.

As a friend of coaches Henson and Collins, and as a reporter trying to cover this sordid mess, I found the whole Bruce Pearl story difficult to digest. I'm one of those who will never forget and never forgive. It isn't fair and it isn't smart to think about it every time I see those black and gold uniforms, but I do.

Chapter 13

Craig Tiley

I have always loved tennis. For years, everyone in our family has played. My wife, Louise, my daughters Chris and Jayne, and my son Dan and I spent countless hours on the courts. So, too, did most of our friends. During the years we lived in Springfield (1962-1980), tennis was the game. A city tournament in Springfield, Decatur, Champaign-Urbana, or Peoria would have a sixty-four draw in men's singles; women's singles, men and women's doubles, and mixed doubles also drew big numbers of players. Eventually, the interest began to die out as more and more sports, especially soccer and golf, attracted young people. Today tennis is still being played and tournaments are still held in central Illinois, but the number of participants is way down.

It is ironic that at the very time tennis participation and interest in the sport waned among the general public, tennis at the University of Illinois began to soar. It began when Craig Tiley was hired to coach the men's team.

Tiley was named interim coach in 1993 and head coach in 1994. The native South African inherited a team that won no Big Ten matches in 1993.

I first met Tiley in 1993 and was fascinated by his goals. As we watched the 1993 team struggle, Tiley said to me, "If I am named head coach, I have a plan that will result in the

University of Illinois becoming a national power in collegiate tennis. We will dominate the Big Ten and compete each year for the national title."

I thought to myself, "Now here's a guy who has been out in the sun too long." But he was so likeable, so energetic, and so positive that I immediately began to pull for him and support him in any way I could.

During his tenure at Illinois, Tiley has proven to be the best recruiter and best coach of Ron Guenther's entire stable of fine coaches. Tiley is well connected in international tennis circles, and he began to convince a host of nationally ranked young players that they should come to the University of Illinois and play for the Illini. This is not an easy selling job. Although Tiley does have a great tennis facility (the Atkins Tennis Center), there are not many other reasons for the great young players to pick Illinois over the Stanfords and Georgias of the collegiate tennis world. The only conclusion that can be reached is that the blue-chippers come to Illinois because of Craig Tiley.

His teams won fifty-seven consecutive Big Ten matches in regular season and tournament play between 1997 and 2001. His teams have twice advanced to the finals of the ITA National Indoor Championships and have reached the NCAA Elite Eight on two occasions. He has produced one or more All-Americans each year since 1998, including Cary Frankin and Graydon Oliver, Illinois' first-ever national doubles champions.

Tiley's players have been named All-Americans sixteen times, including thirteen over the last five seasons.

Tiley has also served as captain of the South Africa Davis Cup team since 1999, and was named the National Coach of the Year in collegiate tennis that same year.

Tiley came to the U of I as the Director of Instruction at Atkins. When former coach Neil Adams left, Tiley was named interim coach and then head coach. Prior to coming to Illinois, Tiley worked with several of the top teaching professionals in the world including Vic Braden, Dennis Van der Meer, Steve Smith, and Harry Hopman. In addition to his duties at Illinois and with the South Africa Davis Cup team, Tiley also coaches several of the world's touring pros.

Tiley is always looking for new challenges.

He came to me one day and said he wanted to bring a professional tournament to Champaign-Urbana. This was a long shot, but I told him I would help promote it on the air. I had no doubts this time that he would get the job done, and he did. The USTA Challenger, the largest professional tournament in Illinois, has been a fixture at Atkins for the past several years.

What do others think of Tiley?

"No one is a better example of toughness, class, and bringing a program from the bottom up than Craig Tiley," says Stanford Coach Dick Gould.

"Craig is a hard worker and always does things in a first-class manner. Without a doubt, he's one of the best in the NCAA," agrees Florida Coach Andy Jackson.

There is no question in my mind that what Tiley has accomplished at the University of Illinois, in a relatively short period of time, has to go down in the Illini history books as one of the best coaching jobs ever. I am proud to have Craig Tiley as a friend. For those who love tennis, he has brought us countless thrills. When you get a chance, go watch his teams play.

Chapter 14

Mike Hebert

One of the nicest things an athlete ever said to me came from an unlikely source: Melissa Beitz, an All-Big Ten setter for Coach Don Hardin's Illini volleyball team.

I had written the epilogue for Mike Pearson's book, *Illini Legends, Lists & Lore*, in which I described how much I loved the University of Illinois and its athletic teams.

"One of the reasons I came to the University of Illinois was because of what you wrote in that book. I was leaning toward Illinois, but when I read that I knew it was the right place for me," said Melissa, who had starred at Stewardson-Strasburg High School before deciding to become an Illini.

She told me that early in her career, and I was really stunned. I thanked her and gave her a little hug. From that time until she graduated, she was one of my favorite Illini. Little things mean a lot.

In that epilogue, I had written about a lot of reasons why I loved Illinois so much including volleyball coach Mike Hebert.

One Monday noon at our Champaign Rotary Club meeting, Mike Hebert was introduced as the featured speaker. He had been named women's volleyball coach at Illinois and his mission now was to educate us. He was trying to drum up some enthusiasm for a game that most of us had played at picnics in the park. Mike began his speech by saying, "This is a volleyball." We laughed at that. Then we began to learn. We began to watch. One of the greatest pleasures I've had at Illinois was watching Mike's team rise to national prominence, lead the nation in attendance, and provide thrilling season after season. Mary (Eggers), Nancy (Brookhart), Kirsten (Gleis)– what a wonderful ride!

Hebert is no longer at Illinois. He left about the same time that Theresa Grentz was named head coach of the women's basketball team. I think Mike felt that there was not going to be room for the two of them at the same university, and that the fantastic support for volleyball might be diminished as fans of women's sports chose between volleyball and basketball. Hebert is now the very successful head coach at the University of Minnesota.

Hebert and his successor at Illinois, Don Hardin, are two of the most interesting coaches I have ever been around. They are bright, articulate, well read, and always willing to talk outside the "sports box" on a variety of subjects. It has been such a treat to have them on our "Saturday Sportsline" shows. At the conclusion of our conversations with them, my co-host Loren Tate and I just sit back and smile. There is great satisfaction in being part of stimulating dialogue.

I would recommend reading Hebert's book, *Mike Hebert –The Fire Still Burns*, published in 1993. I re-read the book this past April, and it reminded me once again of how fascinating Hebert is and how much I miss being around him and his wife Sherry.

In the book's acknowledgments section, Hebert writes about the involvement of Jack Whitman, former sales manager at WDWS and WHMS radio in Champaign, and myself as station manager in getting Illinois volleyball on the radio.

There weren't many stations carrying volleyball games on the radio, but we sent Mike Kelly out to do it. It mattered little that Kelly was totally unfamiliar with volleyball and hadn't the slightest idea how to do play-by-play of it. (Neither did the rest of us, of course.) But we could tell that Hebert and his program were going to be big winners on our campus, and we wanted to be a part of it.

Kelly, who is now the radio voice of the University of Missouri, quickly learned the ropes (with the help of Hebert), and we were off and running, proud to be part of a real "happening" at the U of I. When Kelly left our stations for KMOX in St. Louis, the volleyball play-by-play job went to Dave Loane, who not only played volleyball himself but also knew how to do exciting play-by-play from day one. Loane is still doing volleyball for WDWS as well as for FoxTV. Our relationship with the Illini volleyball program has been terrific all these years, but I don't know if there would have been game one on the radio without Hebert.

Hebert's book explains his first look at Kenney Gym, where his teams would later play fantastic volleyball and turn the game into the hottest ticket in town.

"Kenney Gym was the worst facility I had ever seen or heard about. We had no locker room, but that was the least of our problems. The place was filthy, scum everywhere. There were pads around the girders that were nothing but coat hangars wrapped around old mattresses. We found maggots crawling in every one of them. Windows were broken out of the gym, leaves were scattered everywhere and the floor hadn't had any attention in who knows how many decades. There was stuff hanging on the walls that I can't describe because I can't begin to guess what it was.

"Don and I looked at each other (Hardin was Hebert's assistant coach at the time) and we didn't know whether to laugh or cry. We had nothing. No ball, no net, no place to store anything securely if we'd had a ball and a net."

Things finally worked out, the coaches got it going, and, as they say, the rest is history. Hebert, Hardin and the players they recruited put Illinois on the volleyball map to stay. Hardin later left the program for his own head coaching job at Louisville, then returned as head coach when Hebert left for Minnesota.

In Hebert's book, there is a great story about his conversation with Karol Kahrs, who was running the women's athletic program at the time, and who hired Mike. The conversation had to do with whether he and Sherry would be married right away or simply live together when they got to Champaign:

"That was a completely normal conversation to have where I was living, but Karol practically choked on her cereal. She was utterly knocked off balance by the fact that a coach would come in and live with a woman without being married.

"Ultimately, Sherry made an honest man of me, marrying me in 1984 on the president's lawn at the U of I. We had our reception in the Varsity Room. Now, finally, we were respectable, living in sin no longer."

Mike and Sherry, I miss you guys.

Chapter 15

John Mackovic

Not many people liked John Mackovic.

He was too arrogant for central Illinois, too slick, too dapper. He made people uncomfortable when he was around them. He liked wine. Never hung out with people at the Tumble Inn. Didn't drink beer. Didn't backslap. And glory be, never wore orange.

Yet he built Illinois into a real contender. All four of his Illinois teams played in bowl games. In four years his Illini teams won thirty, lost sixteen, and tied one. It was a winning percentage, better than most. He was Big Ten Coach of the Year in his first two seasons. His 1989 team won ten games, and his 1990 team tied for the Big Ten championship.

In an amazing decision by University Chancellor Mort Weir, Mackovic was named athletic director on December 23, 1988. He held both the AD and head football coach jobs until 1991, when he suddenly bolted for Texas. He left just before the Illini were to play in the 1991 John Hancock Bowl.

There is little doubt that Mackovic had no business being both AD and football coach. He did little as AD, and it was not until Ron Guenther took over that positive things began to happen: new facilities were built, top-flight coaches were hired, fundraising soared, and Illinois became competitive at nearly every level in nearly every sport.

Mackovic had his own reasons for leaving for Texas. I believe the main one was that he had decided there was no way he was going to win a national championship at Illinois and that his chances of doing so at Texas were pretty good.

One night we were playing basketball at Texas, and Mackovic was there. He was wearing cowboy boots, and he stood up and gave the "Hook 'em, Horns" sign when the school song was played. We couldn't believe our eyes. The sophisticate had gone country, at least for a while.

Texas soon got fed up with Mackovic. Not so much for his sophistication, but for his losing. His Texas teams never quite lived up to the expectations of their fans, and Mackovic was gone. Texas likes to win. If you don't win, it doesn't matter if you are John Mackovic or Billy Bob Thornton–you are outta there.

One afternoon–after Illinois had won a Homecoming game–Mackovic and his friends from Kansas City showed up at the U of I Alumni Association party. The executive director of the Alumni Association, Lou Liay, had invited them.

After being introduced by Liay and receiving a rousing ovation from the happy alums in the audience, Mackovic said:

"I see this is a high-class party." He reached over and pulled out a jug of wine and held it high. "I think my friends and I will have to wait until we get home to uncork some of the good stuff."

I believe he meant it as a joke. It was always hard to tell when John was telling a joke. But there was not even a snicker when he said that. In fact, several people began whispering to each other: "See, I told you about him. He's such a snob."

Not many tears were shed when Mackovic left for Texas.

He reappeared after the dismissal at Texas as an in-studio television commentator on college football games. I thought he was getting better and better at it with each passing week, but the coaching bug got him again and he is now the head football coach at Arizona.

On the other hand, people just loved John's wife, Arlene. She was and is everything John is not. Arlene is fun to be around and just as down to earth as anyone you'll ever meet. When the Mackovics moved to Texas, they left Arlene's father in Champaign because he was getting such special treatment here. When she came to Champaign, she would stop by WDWS every time, just to say hello. Arlene was also a frequent participant in Operation Rainbow, assisting a team of physicians on trips to various locales to help young children in need of medical treatment.

One final John Mackovic story:

The first year he was in town, I went to his office to get him to sign a contract that committed him to certain radio shows on WDWS. He looked at the contract, which had all the numbers filled in. He then laid it aside and asked, "Do you like baseball?"

"Sure I do," I replied.

He grabbed the contract and headed out the door with me following. We walked over to an Illinois game and sat down in the private booth in the press box. Mackovic laid the contract down between us but never said a word about it. We watched several innings and made small talk. The contract just lay there between us. He asked no questions about it, said nothing about the amount of money I was proposing to pay him. It was very strange. And intimidating, which is what he wanted.

Finally, he jumped to his feet and said, "I have to go. I have a meeting."

I stood up too, not knowing what to do next and not knowing what to say about the contract. At that point, he reached into his pocket and pulled out the most expensive-looking pen I had ever seen and scrawled his name on the contract.

"Thank you very much," I said.

He never replied. Just walked out of the booth.

John Mackovic had a way of making you feel very inferior. I have never been around another coach like that, before or since.

He is obviously a very good football coach with a great offensive mind. I wish him well. Perhaps he has lightened up a bit by now. I haven't spoken to him for years, but my experience with him while he was at Illinois was not enjoyable.

The biggest mistake Mackovic made at Illinois was his continual reference to former Michigan Coach Bo Schembechler, a man he admired and tried to emulate. That did not fly in Illini-land. At one meeting of the Quarterback Club, Mackovic began lauding Bo from the podium and members of the audience actually began to boo and hiss. This was Mackovic's *own* booster club that was doing this. Illinois booster clubs are tolerant of most anything–even 0-11 seasons–but don't tell them that Bo Schembechler is someone to be admired.

Chapter 16

Lee Eilbracht

Mike Cummings didn't like to hustle.

The center fielder for the Springfield Caps in the Central Illinois Collegiate League in the late 1960s was a good fielder and a fair hitter, but he was extremely lazy. Some days he was a streak; most days he played like he was mired in the mud.

The coach of the Caps was my good friend Lee Eilbracht, who was a star player and later coach of the Fighting Illini baseball team. Eilbracht won baseball letters in 1943, 1946, and 1947, won the Big Ten batting title in 1946, and coached the Illini from 1952 to 1978. His record was 518-383-6, including four Big Ten titles.

One sunny afternoon during a game at Bloomington-Normal, Eilbracht had enough of Cummings' laziness. After the center fielder loped in and let a ball that he should have caught drop in front of him for a single, Eilbracht called time out.

I was watching the game with my buddy, Frank "Beaver" Schwartz, who had been a star pitcher for the Illini in 1955, 1957, and 1958. Schwartz and I were members of the Board of Directors of the Springfield Caps, and we were instrumental in getting Eilbracht hired as coach.

Schwartz and I just assumed that when Eilbracht called time out that he was going to the mound to have a few words with his pitcher. Not so. The coach walked very slowly from the dugout, past the mound, past second base, all the way into center field where he proceeded to have a nose-to-nose conversation with Cummings. On second thought, it wasn't really a conversation because Eilbracht was doing all the talking and Cummings was doing all the listening.

And Eilbracht continued to talk, and talk, and talk. The game was being held up, of course, and the Bloomington-Normal coach, Denny Bridges (long-time coach at Illinois Wesleyan) came storming out of his dugout and charged the home plate umpire demanding, "What in the _____ is going on out there??"

I have to admit that in all the baseball games I have seen and broadcast, I never saw a coach stop a game and walk out and talk to his center fielder. I thought it was hilarious. Then the Bloomington-Normal fans got into the act. They began booing and yelling at Eilbracht. Finally, Eilbracht turned and walked slowly back from center field to the Caps dugout, and the game resumed.

I don't know what Eilbracht said to Cummings, but from then on Cummings was Mr. Hustle, running to the walls to make spectacular catches, stealing bases, and getting his fair share of hits. And the Caps won the championship.

I got to know Eilbracht during my student days at Illinois when I broadcast the Illini baseball games on WILL. The games were played at old Illinois Field in those days (now the site of the Beckman Institute at Wright and University), and there was no press box. I shared many of the broadcasts with Dave Baum, a superb radio man who now works for "The Score" in Chicago. There were many cold and rainy afternoons when Dave and I would huddle under a tarp, clad in parkas and mittens, singing the praises of the Illini. It was a miserable existence–and we loved every minute.

Eilbracht invited me to take the southern spring trips with the team, and I was able to go on two occasions. The first was to the Memphis Naval Air Station, where the team was quartered in barracks. The coach, the *Courier's* sports editor Bert Bertine, and I stayed in officer's quarters. I sent some stories back to the *News-Gazette*, but mostly I was just there to watch the games and have fun. And it *was* fun. Just hanging out with the players, watching the games, enjoying the sunshine. For an undergrad just back from Korea, it was a little piece of heaven.

The second trip I went on was to Florida State, where the team stayed at a camp built around a lake; the players swam and fished in the lake between games. One night at dinner, Jack Delveaux decided to play a trick on the waitress.

Delveaux, who was a letter winner in both baseball and football at Illinois in the late 1950s, was a great practical joker. When the waitress approached his table, Delveaux stuck out his tongue at her. On his tongue was a dead fish he had found in the lake. The waitress screamed and dropped her tray of dishes. The players had a good laugh over that. Somehow I don't think players in the year 2002 are having *that* much fun.

I loved being around those guys: Gary Kolb (1960), Ethan Blackaby (1960), Ernie Kumerow (1959-61), Jim Vermette (1958-59), and Frank Schwartz (1956-58) were all particular favorites of mine.

Blackaby once managed the Phoenix team when it was in the minors; The team was owned by former Illini basketball star Dave Downey. Vermette was a long time executive director of the University of Illinois Alumni Association. Kumerow got a lot of publicity when he married Marie Accardo, the daughter of Chicago legend Tony Accardo. Even today, Ernie can tell you some stories that someone should use in a book.

I am pleased that my wife and I still consider Lee Eilbracht and his wife, Euline, personal friends. We are all members of the First Presbyterian Church in Champaign.

For many years, Lee did an outstanding job as color commentator on the Illini baseball broadcasts on WDWS while Dave Loane handled the play-by-play. Lee still serves as a "coach-consultant" for major league baseball teams, and he worked this past spring with the Diamondbacks, owned by former Illini Jerry Colangelo.

Chapter 17

Lon Kruger

The stern-wheeler was drifting along at about five mph somewhere on the Columbia or Snake river–I forget exactly where–but I remember the phone call well. It was from Steve Khachaturian at WDWS.

My wife and I had been on the rivers for several days, along with Frank and Pat Van Matre and Kenny and Barbara Berger. It was an easy place to forget the goings-on in the outside world, and phone calls were almost impossible to make or receive unless you were in port. But somehow Steve got through to me; I think he told them it was an emergency.

As it turned out, it wasn't an emergency, but it was a shock.

"Lon Kruger has been trying to get in touch with you all day," Steve said.

"Why?" I wondered.

"He's going to Atlanta to take over the Hawks and he wanted you to know before you found out on television or in the papers," Steve replied.

Luckily I wasn't out on deck, or I might have fallen overboard. Or jumped.

When we left Champaign for the river trip, Michigan State's Tom Izzo was the name being mentioned for Atlanta. Not Kruger.

I never thought that Kruger was long-term at Illinois. The NBA was a goal of his, sometime down the road. I just didn't expect it that soon.

Kruger coached four years at Illinois. His teams won one Big Ten title, appeared in three NCAA tournaments, had an overall record of 81-48, and were 38-28 in the conference. He was considered one of the best young coaches in America and was always going to be in demand.

The fact that Lon tried to let me know personally about the move before the announcement was made was typical of Kruger. He is a kind, thoughtful, generous man. A gentleman in every sense of the word. His wife, Barb, is a perfect match for Lon. Together they immersed themselves into the Champaign-Urbana community just as they had in Gainesville, where Lon coached the Florida Gators for six years prior to coming to Illinois.

After I got back from the river trip and before Lon left for Atlanta, he asked me to lunch at TGI Friday's, just the two of us. He said how appreciative he was of what the radio stations and I personally had done for him and the program. I told him sincerely that he was one of the most cooperative coaches I had ever worked with.

Lon was always easy going, laid back. A pleasure to be around. I told him I was going to miss him, and I meant every word.

Lon's dad died while Lon was at Illinois. Kruger made several trips to Kansas to visit his dad while he was seriously ill. Lon and his dad were very close. When he came back from Kansas, I'd ask him how his dad was doing. At one point Lon said, "We had a good talk this time. He is ready to go."

Shortly thereafter, at an Illini practice at the Assembly Hall, Barb came onto the court and spoke to Lon. They walked back down the tunnel, hand in hand. I never knew for sure, but I've always assumed that was when she told Lon that his dad had died.

During our lunch, I told Lon that my dad had died suddenly at age 50. He said he was very sorry. We agreed that each day should be lived to the fullest. You just never know. When the lunch was over, we shook hands and said goodbye. It was the last time I saw him in person. I catch a glimpse now and then of Lon on television. He wears a tie. At Illinois he made the mock turtleneck the style of the day. His original contract at Atlanta was for $2 million a year. It was a good move for the Krugers, but NBA coaches go through a revolving door. I wish Lon and Barb the best. They deserve it.

Kruger's Big Ten championship team had no NBA prospects, but it was a fun team to watch and to be around: Jerry Gee, Jerry Hester, Brian Johnson, Matt Heldman, and Kevin Turner.

One of the most memorable shots that year was a spinning 360-degree banker by Turner at Wisconsin, which sent the game into overtime. Illinois eventually won 53-47, a rare win in Madison. Following that heart-stopper, the Illini beat Michigan State, Northwestern, Iowa, and Indiana. A 75-72 loss at Purdue was the only blemish in the final eleven games of that 1997-1998 championship season.

Kruger's next team slipped badly to 14-18 overall and 3-13 in the conference. But they rallied during Lon's final season to finish 22-10 and 11-5.

The disappointment of Kruger's departure was quickly alleviated when Ron Guenther hired another of the nation's highly regarded young coaches, Bill Self, as Kruger's replacement.

Self's teams won back-to-back Big Ten titles his first two years.

Self, too, is not considered a long-termer. He is such a hot property that it would not be surprising to see him make a move to another top-level college job or the NBA. More about Self beginning in Chapter 24.

Chapter 18

Ron Turner

Luke Butkus was on the phone. It was another recruiting call. The All-Stater from Bloom Township was used to it by now. Universities from all around the nation were hoping to land him. He was listening intently this time, because it was the University of Illinois calling. Other members of the Butkus family had had some success at Illinois, and Luke wanted to find out what this new coach had to say.

The new coach was Ron Turner, who had been serving as offensive coordinator for the Chicago Bears for the past four years. Turner was hired at Illinois on December 2, 1996. Since the Bears still had a few games left on their schedule, Turner worked both jobs for several weeks.

He would work on Illinois business from 5 a.m. to 6:30 a.m., and then he'd work on Bears business the rest of the day. Late at night it was back to Illinois business, which included recruiting players and a coaching staff. It was a hectic time.

Turner knew how important it was to land Luke Butkus and others like him. The talent level at Illinois when Turner took over was dismal. The old cliché that "you win with good players" is obviously true, and Illinois had but a few in 1996.

Turner made several trips back and forth between Chicago and Champaign as he worked both jobs. He was in his

Illinois office on the weekend he was talking to Butkus on the phone.

Here's the irony: Butkus was also in Champaign. In fact, he was also in the Illini football office, in an assistant coach's office just two doors down from Turner! In another of its many bizarre rulings over the years, the NCAA had ruled that since Turner was still working for the Bears, and even though he had already signed a contract with the U of I, he could not speak to prospective student athletes in person. It was okay to talk to them on the phone.

So as the recruits made their official visits, they were brought to the football coaches' complex and handed a telephone to talk to the head coach who was just a few feet away. Turner recalls talking to ten or twelve recruits on the phone.

"It was really very strange. We had to explain to the kids what was happening, that it was the NCAA rules that kept me from seeing them in person. Ironically, we wound up getting most of them, so it worked out, but I never want to go through that again."

The most awkward time was when Turner hung up with Butkus and walked out into the hallway. Butkus walked out at the same time. They stood looking at each other for a brief moment before Turner turned around and walked back into his office without saying a word to Butkus.

"I was so conscious of not breaking the rules that I did a quick one-eighty and went back into my office and never came out again until I had talked to all the recruits on the phone. Crazy!"

Turner said he and Butkus and other fifth-year seniors who were part of that unique experience laughed about it several times during their careers at Illinois.

Butkus, especially, liked to tell other players how Turner "snubbed" him during his official visit.

Turner's first Illinois team didn't win a game. They went 0-11. It was a very long season for everyone, including the announcers. Although there is always an attempt to be upbeat, positive, and energetic on the broadcasts, it is a real challenge when your team gets down–oftentimes *way* down–by halftime. At one point my color commentator, Jim Grabowski, said, "I ran out of positives a long time ago. Now I have about run out of negatives." That from as loyal an Illini as you can find! It was just one of those seasons.

In 1998, some progress was made. Turner's team went 3-8.

In 1999, all kinds of good things happened and the Illini finished 8-4, including a win over Virginia in the Micronpc.com Bowl in Miami. The final score was 63-21, which included a touchdown pass from wide receiver Brandon Lloyd to quarterback Kurt Kittner. Kittner promptly drew a flag as he flung the ball into the stands. Man, that was fun! I would rank that game right up near the top of the really enjoyable times I've had in the booth. The 0-11 season seemed a million miles away that night.

Turner's team slipped back to 5-6 in 2000 and left people wondering where the program was. Were we going back down? Were we really ever up? Were we going to be a player or a pretender in the Big 10 conference? No one knew for sure as Turner prepared his team for 2001.

A lot of questions were answered in 2001 as the Illini won an undisputed Big Ten title and got to a BCS game. Top eight in the nation. The disappointing loss to LSU in the Sugar Bowl did little to dampen the enthusiasm for the 2002 season.

And to think that it all started when Ron Turner began phoning recruits who were sitting in an office just down the hall from him. Talk about humble beginnings.

I consider myself very fortunate to have worked with and been around such high-class people as Ron and Wendy Turner. You hear horror stories from other announcers at other universities about their relationships with coaches. Ron and Wendy and their kids are a credit to this university and this community. The way they are makes it so easy to be on their side–to hope that good things happen to them.

And I do hope so.

As president of the American Business Club in Springfield, I presented an Illinois poster to Coach Bob Blackman in 1971, his first year at Illinois.

Louise and I pose with Mrs. Marajen Stevick Chinigo (middle), owner of *The News-Gazette* and WDWS/WHMS, in 1980. It was my first day as vice president and general manager of the radio stations.

Jerry Lewis cracked me up in Las Vegas while we were preparing for the muscular dystrophy telethon in 1978.

In 1997, Lon Kruger was the featured speaker at the Developmental Services Banquet. I was MC for the event.

At the Illini basketball banquet with the five seniors. Left to right, Lucas Johnson, Robert Archibald, Frank Williams, Damir Krupalija, and Cory Bradford.

I interviewed Mary Lou Retton at the U of I's Women's Conference in 2000.

With Bela Karolyi after I interviewed him on "Penny for Your Thoughts."

With my family at the Summer Olympics in Atlanta in 1996. My daughter Jayne, second from left, was Director of Aquatics for the Olympics.

Intently watching water polo with the broadcast crew at the 1996 Summer Olympics in Atlanta. I did the play-by-play for One-on-One Sports.

Roger Ebert did an interview on PFYT in April 2001 when he was in town for his Overlooked Film Festival.

The students made the broadcast team honorary members of Orange Krush in 2001. Loren Tate is on the left, and Ed Bond is on the right.

Illini quarterback Kurt Kittner and me with the 2001 Big Ten championship trophy.

Visiting St. Petersburg, Russia in 1992 with Illini coach Lou Henson.

With Loren Tate (left) and Lou Henson at my birthday party in 1987.

Posing with Loren Tate (left) and football coach Mike White.

I was named an honorary Varsity "I" member in 1979. I am with former Illini (left to right) Frank Schwartz, Bill Ridley, and Russ Martin.

My daughter Chris Lukeman (kneeling) is the athletic director at Countryside School in Champaign. I visited with Illini players and an Illini majorette on Sports Day in 2001.

I was presented with the Illini Legend Award in 1999 by the Quarterback Club. I'm with Roger Huddleston (left) and Ron Turner.

With women's basketball coach Theresa Grentz at the Developmental Services banquet in 1998.

With Jack Kemp after a PFYT interview.

Posing with long-time Champaign Central football coach Tom Stewart. I did high school broadcasts on WDWS.

Illini football coach Lou Tepper and I were honored at the Fellowship for Christian Athletes banquet in 1996. From left to right, Lou Tepper, FCA director Tim Johnson, and myself.

With wheelchair Olympian Jean Driscoll at the Champaign Park District's Olympic tribute in 1996.

With Monsignor Edward Duncan, who is the long-time chaplain for the U of I teams.

I interviewed Tippi Hendren, star of Alfred Hitchcock's *The Birds* on PFYT.

With Dick Vitale, prior to the event where he stood on his head at Assembly Hall after losing a bet with me that the Illini would get to the Final Four in 1989.

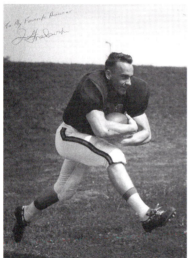

Jim Grabowski in his Illini days as a fullback. He did color commentary with me on the Illini Sports Network for years.

My wife Louise with Deon Thomas (left) and Steve Roth in Russia in 1992.

Chapter 19

Theresa Grentz

It takes six pages in the U of I women's basketball press guide to tell of Theresa Grentz and her accomplishments. The resume begins in 1972, when Grentz helped Immaculata beat West Chester State 52-48 in the first-ever AIAW national title game for women's basketball. It ends in 2001 with her induction into the Women's Basketball Hall of Fame. This woman has done a lot to be proud of.

My time with Theresa has me baffled.

Let me explain. When she first burst upon the scene at Illinois, she was the talk of the town, of the state, of the women's world of collegiate basketball.

I was stunned the first time I heard her speak by her ability to tell stories, make cogent points and entertain the audience. She was a big hit wherever she went. The press guide estimates that she has made more than 800 public appearances in her seven years at Illinois. She has her own television and radio shows, and during the 2001-2002 season, she spoke at dozens of schools in the Champaign-Urbana area.

Early on she began to call me "The Silver Fox" because of my hair color. I was delighted. It was fun. She was fun, and we had a good time. I had the pleasure of lining her up as a speaker for the Developmental Services Center's annual recognition dinner, and I introduced her. She was fantastic at the podium, as usual.

When Stevie Jay (WDWS morning host) and his wife Janet were home after the birth of their triplets, Grentz filled in for Stevie every morning for a week. She was a big hit. People loved to hear her joke around with the audience and station personnel. I greeted her every morning at the station, and our relationship was terrific.

Somewhere along the way, something changed. I still don't know exactly what.

For the last few months of my play-by-play broadcasting career, the coach would barely speak when we met. She went only reluctantly on "Saturday Sportsline," and when she did come on, the conversation was stiff and not very informative or productive.

I believe the trouble started when Allison Curtin quit the team and transferred to Tulsa. Curtin became the twelfth player to leave Grentz's program: Grentz and her staff had recruited six of those twelve players, including Curtin.

I was one of many reporters who covered the story, and it was talked about extensively on my morning show, "Penny for Your Thoughts," as well as on "Saturday Sportsline." Curtin's departure got people's tongues wagging, including mine. Curtin was one of the most popular players ever recruited at Illinois, and her following, especially from her hometown of Taylorville, was tremendous. People wanted to know what was going on with women's basketball when a player like Curtin left the program.

While admitting that none of us knew the behind-the-scenes story and were not privy to private meetings and practices, I took the position that something was wrong when twelve players bailed out. Even the transfer of Anne O'Neil, one of the most talented recruits in the country, didn't affect Illinois fans as much as Curtin's leaving did.

Dave Loane, the sports director at WDWS and the play-by-play voice of women's basketball, called Curtin and interviewed her on the air. Grentz was on an overseas trip with the team when Curtin left. The coach didn't like the fact that Loane called Curtin, and she didn't like the fact that I talked about it on the air. I don't know what she thought about the many other members of the media who covered the story in much the same manner.

Grentz never once said anything to me about the Curtin story. I can only guess that this is what changed our relationship.

Grentz's first team at Illinois in 1995-96 went 13-15. She followed that with her two best seasons: 24-8 in 1996-97 and 20-10 in 1997-98. Both teams were ranked in the nation's top fifteen and both reached the NCAA Sweet Sixteen. The 1996-97 team, led by Ashley Berggren, was the Big Ten champion. Berggren was named the Big Ten Player of the Year, the first Illinois player to be so honored. Grentz was named Big Ten Coach of the Year both years.

Last year (2001-2002), a young Illini team struggled, attendance was down, and the player defections lingered in the minds of many Illinois fans.

I sincerely hope that Grentz and her wonderful staff can get the Illini back on track in 2002-03. It's going to take a lot to draw big crowds to Assembly Hall, which is much too large of an arena for women's basketball in Illinois right now. Good luck, Theresa!

Chapter 20

Ray Eliot

It was October 27, 1956. Illini coach Ray Eliot had invited some people to stop by his house on Springfield Avenue in Champaign to celebrate Illinois' 20-13 upset of No. 1-ranked Michigan State earlier in the day.

I didn't know Ray well at that time and had gotten my invitation via Larry Stewart, who was the WDWS radio station manager and my boss. It didn't matter to Ray. He treated everyone the same. Old friends, new friends, strangers, he slapped everyone on the back and greeted them with a big smile. He always reminded me of a big bear. A big, gentle, loveable bear.

When he came to me, he put his arm around my shoulders, smiled, and said, "You like that game, son?"

I was one year into classes at the U of I, just back from a two-year stint in Korea, and as green and naive as a rookie reporter could be. I was in heaven. Here was Ray Eliot talking to me!

"Yes sir," I think I replied.

"Me too! Me too!" Ray shouted, waving his arms and moving on to greet another lucky person.

It was his thing, upsetting No. 1 teams. He had done it against Michigan just the year before. You could always count on Eliot's teams pulling a big upset almost every year. Many times those upsets occurred during the homecoming game.

On that memorable afternoon, Abe Woodson had scored three touchdowns in the second half as the Illini rallied from a 13-0 halftime deficit to win 20-13. Woodson scored on a two-yard touchdown plunge to cut it to 13-6 midway into the third quarter. Then he tied the game on a seventy-yard run in the fourth quarter. Later, as the game wound down, Woodson took a screen pass from Illini quarterback Bill Offenbecher at the Illinois eighteen-yard line and went all the way for the winning touchdown, eluding some tacklers and hurdling over others.

I will always remember Ray Eliot for his kindness to me. Here was a legendary football coach who took time to talk to a young guy who was trying to prepare himself for a play-by-play job. He didn't have to, but he did.

I will always remember Ray Eliot for his ability to weave Illini stories into his heart-stopping, tear-jerking speeches. I never had the privilege of being in the locker room when he spoke to his teams, but I heard Ray dozens of times at civic clubs, at conventions, and at meetings of the Quarterback Club. He was a master at delivering a message. It is no wonder that he was able to motivate his Illinois teams. We all wanted to go out and hit someone after hearing Ray speak.

Stories about Ray Eliot live on yet today. His not-so-good eyesight was the subject of many Eliot stories. One had to do with Illini quarterback John Easterbrook. It is said that during a game in which nothing was going well, Eliot turned to his team, looked up and down the line of players and shouted, "What's going on out there? Easterbrook, get in there!" The coach waited. Nothing happened. He repeated, "Easterbrook, I said get in there!" Nothing happened. Finally, an assistant coach walked up to Eliot and whispered to him, "Coach, Easterbrook has *been* in there, and he's *still* in there."

Stewart told me that the first time Eliot came to the broadcast booth to do their initial broadcast on the Purity Sunbeam Football Network, they were both in for a big surprise.

"You know, I've never seen a game from up here, not even a practice session," Eliot remarked.

Stewart replied, "Don't worry, there's nothing to it. I've got charts and everything prepared. I'll ask you some questions at first, while we get the feel of it. After that you can jump in whenever you want to. You'll be fine."

Stewart began the play-by-play, and at the appropriate time he asked Eliot about a certain player. "How's he playing?" There was no answer from Eliot.

Minutes later Stewart asked another question, about a different player. There was no answer from Eliot.

Finally, at the first commercial break, Stewart said, "What's the matter, Ray? I asked you some questions about a couple of players and you didn't say anything." To which Eliot replied, "You mean to tell me that you can read those numbers from up here?"

Somehow they got it worked out. Maybe Ray got some better glasses, I don't know. But he and Stewart were broadcast partners for many happy years. I had the great pleasure of joining them in the booth at a later date. Stewart would do the play-by-play of the first and fourth quarters, and I'd do the second and third.

Eliot coached at Illinois for eighteen years. His record was a modest 83-73-11. But his teams won Big Ten championships in 1946, 1951, and 1953 and Rose Bowl titles in 1947 and 1952.

And the man will never be forgotten. His speech, "The Proper State of Mind," was recorded and has been enjoyed by the followers of football worldwide. If you just read the words to that speech, it would be just a so-so speech, but when you listened to Ray Eliot deliver it, with his special heartfelt emotion, those of us who wear the orange and blue cry every time. It is so beautiful. Just like the man himself.

Chapter 21

Rob Judson

Sitting in Rob Judson's office at the Ubben Center, my attention was immediately drawn to something that I had never seen in a coach's office anywhere else: a bookcase filled with history books.

Oh, there were some basketball books in there too, mostly motivational types written by people like Phil Jackson and Bill Bradley. But for the most part, the bookcase was jammed with writings about or by Teddy Roosevelt and other historical figures whom Judson admires. There were some Stephen Ambrose books as well, about D-Day, World War II, and the Lewis and Clark expedition. During Judson's last year at Illinois, he and I were both reading Ambrose's *Nothing Like It In the World*, about the men who built the transcontinental railroad from 1863 to 1869.

Jud gave me a head's-up to one of the finest books I've ever read about young people and basketball. It's called *Counting Coup* by Larry Holton. It tells of the time Holton spent on an Indian reservation writing about a female Native American basketball team. Jud and I had a great time discussing this book, and I would highly recommend it to anyone who is interested in young people and basketball.

I made frequent trips to Jud's office to record the assistant coaches' show, which ran before every Illinois broadcast.

We alternated shows between all the assistant coaches, and it was a duty that I enjoyed very much. It was sort of "my time" with the assistants in both basketball and football. Invariably, after our interview was completed, Jud would say, "What are you reading now, Turp?"

I'd tell him, and if I were reading a mystery–such as one by my favorite mystery writers James Lee Burke and Tony Hillerman, Jud wouldn't show much interest.

But if the topic was history, he would want to know everything about the book right then and there. Jud was particularly impressed when I did two interviews with Stephen Ambrose on "Penny for Your Thoughts."

On long road trips when the lights were turned down and most everyone on board was asleep, I would see Jud's light on, and he'd be reading something, usually about history or religion. I'd have a book open, too. It was a special kinship that I felt with Jud, although I have no idea whether he shared it.

Jud was a history major at Illinois and taught high school history in addition to coaching basketball. He moved on to the college ranks as an assistant coach at Northern Illinois University, assistant coach at Bradley, assistant coach at Illinois, and is now the head coach at NIU.

Jud's Peoria connections were invaluable in the recruitment of the three Peoria Manual stars, Sergio McClain, Marcus Griffin, and Frank Williams. The trio continued winning championships at Illinois after winning four consecutive state high school titles. Without Judson, it is not clear as to whether the star threesome would have wound up at Illinois.

Judson was one of three assistants to Lon Kruger. The others were Robert McCullum and Steve Henson.

When Kruger left for Atlanta and Bill Self was hired by Ron Guenther, part of the arrangement was that Judson would remain on the staff and Self could bring two assistants with him. Judson spent several days deciding whether he would stay or not. It was not that Judson wanted to leave, but he had strong feelings about being one of the two assistants who could go on the road to recruit. He felt a strong recruiting reputation would help him in getting a head coaching job within the next couple of years.

Self brought Norm Roberts and Billy "Clyde" Gillespie with him from Tulsa, and both of them were considered fine recruiters as well. Finally, it was worked out:

Judson and Roberts would join Self on the road and Gillespie would work in the office as the recruiting coordinator. It stayed that way until Judson got the NIU job, at which time Self hired former Peoria Manual coach Wayne McClain.

Judson has a long way to go to build the Northern Illinois program. But the NIU people have great confidence in him, as do I. He has the personality, drive, know-how, and coaching ability to be a very successful head coach.

I miss Rob and Kim. I miss, "Hey, Turp, whatcha readin'?"

Section 3

BASKETBALL

Chapter 22

Rod Cardinal

Some thought there must have been a leak in the roof of the dome. Others contended that someone had simply spilled some water on the floor. Whatever happened, it caused Kenny Battle to slip and fall during the shoot-around the day before the Illini were to face Louisville in the NCAA Regional at Minneapolis in 1989. I was standing within ten feet of Battle when it happened; he grabbed his knee and was in obvious pain. My heart sank. Battle was the heart and soul of the Illini team and had played a big role in the first- and second-round games in Indianapolis as Illinois whipped McNeese State 77-71 and Ball State 72-60. To win the regional without Battle was unthinkable.

Long-time Illini trainer Rod Cardinal rushed to Battle and began a quick diagnosis of the injury. After further examination and X-rays, it was determined that the injury was a deep bruise on the inside of the knee. The game against Louisville was twenty-four hours away. Getting Battle ready to play became priority No. 1.

Back at the hotel, Cardinal began to work on the knee. Ice for twenty minutes, then off for forty minutes. That, plus pain medication, became the routine for the next twelve hours; all night long Cardinal followed that regimen. He had a key to

Battle's room, and he went back and forth, back and forth, from dusk to daylight.

At one point, when Cardinal was walking down the hall toward Battle's room, he met Athletic Director John Mackovic. Mackovic, in his subtle way, said, "Doc, our trainer at Wake Forest would stay up all night and get him ready to play." Cardinal, who had already planned to do just that, was now sure that was exactly what he was going to do. Get him ready to play.

Cardinal, Battle, and Battle's roommate, Lowell Hamilton, got virtually no sleep that night. But by morning Battle was feeling better. He walked gingerly on the knee during the game-day shoot-around, which was held in the ballroom of the hotel. It was really more of a walk-through as the Illini went over the scouting report on Louisville. It was determined that Battle could do no more harm to the knee by playing that night; it was only a question of how much pain he could handle. The game was on!

Ironically, Hamilton went down in the first half with a sprained ankle. Now Cardinal had two starters to worry about. Hamilton's injury occurred when he rolled his ankle after stepping on Felton Spencer's foot. Cardinal retaped and tightly wrapped Hamilton's ankle, and he was able to compete at about halfspeed.

With some great help from the bench (Ervin Small, Marcus Liberty, and Larry Smith) the Illini beat Louisville 83-69 to move into the regional final against Syracuse. Cardinal kept Battle loose by installing a stationary bicycle next to the bench; when Coach Henson took Battle out of the game, he immediately got on the bike and started pedaling.

The day after the win was an off day before the regional final, and Cardinal had more time to work on both Battle and Hamilton. He was asked to be interviewed by CBS-

TV's Verne Lundquist. The Illini injuries and their treatment by the Illini trainer had become the big story of this regional final.

The regional final matched two talented teams with future NBA players at nearly every position. The Illini started Battle with Kendall Gill, Nick Anderson, Steve Bardo and Hamilton. Liberty came off the bench. All but Hamilton went on to the NBA. Syracuse started Billy Owens, Sherman Douglas, and Derek Coleman, all future NBA stars. The winner would move on to the Final Four in Seattle.

Early in the game, Gill got smacked in the mouth and began to bleed heavily. Cardinal stopped the bleeding, and Gill played on with the front of his jersey now a bright red. After the game, the doctor snipped a piece of hanging skin from Gill's lip, thinking it was dead skin. Not so. Gill yelped loudly!

But nothing could put a damper on the postgame celebration. Illinois had beaten Syracuse 89-86 and was headed to the Final Four. The walking wounded all played.

In the crowded locker room after the game, the players mingled with the media, friends, and family. It was the happiest scene I can remember in all the years I have been covering Illinois sports. I walked over to Rod Cardinal and whispered in his ear, "Rod Cardinal, MVP!" He smiled and tried to shrug it off. But there is no denying this fact: Illinois wouldn't have made it to the Final Four in 1989 without the work of Rod Cardinal.

Under extreme pressure, he performed his duties magnificently. Rod likes to talk about the "magic" of those two games—the decisions made by Coach Lou and his staff, the performances of the key players and the subs; everything seemed to go right. Rod Cardinal performed some magic of his own, never to be forgotten.

Chapter 23

Basketball 2002

"This is the MASH unit, Rod Cardinal speaking." No one likes to hear excuses. But there has never been an Illini basketball season in which more players missed more practices and more games because of injury than the 2001-02 season.

I wonder how many days Coach Bill Self had everyone available to practice or play. It wouldn't be very many. Self was also a victim, bothered by a bout of diverticulitis and a bad knee. Surgery was discussed for both problems, but the coach stuck it out until the end of the season.

Lucas Johnson, Robert Archibald, Damir Krupalija, Frank Williams, and Brett Melton were all down at one time or another.

Melton missed every game after the Texas A&M Corpus Christi game on December 1, when he went down with one of the worst-looking sprained ankles I have ever seen. He wound up red-shirting.

Johnson had surgery on a torn ACL on his right knee in October. He came back much quicker than anyone imagined, playing in his first game January 23 against Wisconsin. He wore a big brace throughout the rest of the season.

Krupalija was off to a great start and was named the MVP of the Las Vegas tournament before going down with a foot injury. He missed seven games and had not played since December 22 when he, too, returned to action against Wisconsin.

But on February 3, in a game against Michigan, Damir reinjured the foot and had to have surgery. He finally made it back for the Big Ten tournament in early March.

Williams hurt his hand before the season started when he and Brian Cook were trying out for an international team. He practiced and played several games with a wrap on the hand.

Archibald also hurt his right hand and had it heavily wrapped for much of the latter part of the season.

Cardinal and the team physicians, Dr. Robert Gurtler and Dr. Steve Soboroff, were never busier than they were during the 2001-02 season.

The injuries forced Self to play several players out of position, and he scrambled to find the right combinations at times because of the injuries and the unavailability of players. This became a real problem when Archibald and Cook got into early foul trouble, which they did quite often.

On the positive side, freshman center Nick Smith, freshman Roger Powell, and junior college transfer Blandon Ferguson got more playing time than they would have had there been no injuries to key players. All three will be a lot more experienced going into the 2002-03 season. They will surely be needed as the Illini line up next season without Johnson, Archibald, Williams, Krupalija, or Cory Bradford.

Bradford was remarkably durable during his time at Illinois. He started every game of his collegiate career and made a three-pointer in eighty-eight consecutive games, which is an NCAA record. A bad knee hobbled Cory the previous season, but he never missed a game. He would end up fifth in school history for scoring.

Chapter 24

Bill Self

"Hey Turp, come on out here for a minute." The summons by Coach Bill Self to center court at Assembly Hall, where he had his 2001-02 team gathered, came as a big surprise to me. I had just finished doing my pregame interview with Self and was putting on my coat, ready to head home for dinner before coming back for the Penn State game that night. It was to be "Jim Turpin Night," and I needed to put on a clean shirt.

I walked to center court, and Self began to talk. He said some very nice things about me, and then on behalf of the team, he gave me a big, brightly decorated box that contained an Illinois basketball parka and some other Illini gear. It was a generous and totally unexpected gesture on the part of the coach. He said he wanted the presentation to be private and not a part of the pregame festivities set for that night. He also said that he wanted the team to be there when he gave me the gift. It was the closest I came to crying the whole day and night.

Then the coach asked me to say a few words to the team.

I stumbled through a couple of sentences, telling them what a pleasure it had been just being associated with them, and how I hoped that they would have the best of luck for the rest of the season.

Self asked me how long I had been broadcasting games, and I said, "About forty years. None of you guys were even born when I began broadcasting Illinois games."

Always the one to have the last word, Self said, "Hell, I wasn't even born yet."

The team got quite a laugh out of that one.

"Thanks, Turp. We'll see you tonight," the coach said. High fives all around, and I walked off the floor with my big box of goodies. Rod Cardinal was there, and I asked him if he had anything to do with all this. Rod, ever the thoughtful one, just smiled and said he knew that I had always wanted an Illinois basketball parka. Regardless of how that little ceremony came about, it is something I will never forget. Just me, the coach, the guys, and a few words at center court. As they say, priceless!

Bill Self is very difficult to describe in a few words. He is a very complex man, and one of the most intriguing I've ever met. He is a public relations dream. His press conferences, teleconferences, and postgame appearances are not to be missed. He always says frank and interesting things about every aspect of the game, whether it be players, strategy, officials, other coaches, or other teams, it doesn't matter. He never ducks a question and he treats them all as if the questions were well thought out and pertinent, which they often are not. I have heard reporters in Self press conferences ask really dumb questions, and Self will turn those questions into bright, articulate, and meaningful answers. Now that's really a trick, but he is a master at it.

At a meeting of the Rebounders, the men's basketball support group, Self will go on for twenty or thirty minutes without a single note, ad-libbing his way through thought-provoking monologues that are both funny and serious. Oh, he has a couple of phrases that he uses more often than he should ("on the flip side" and "unless I'm mistaken"), but most everything he says is fascinating to his audience. I've heard a lot of coaches, but I truly believe he is the best at delivering off-the-cuff remarks and answering questions.

Self's second season at Illinois was a roller coaster.

The team opened at home with a convincing 76-58 win over a good Gonzaga club, and fans were sure that his highly ranked team was going to live up to expectations. Hey, we might be going to the Final Four!

The Illini went 5-0 while winning the Las Vegas Invitational. A long trip to Maryland after the Vegas tournament was not what the Illini needed to face the eventual national champion Terps. Maryland won 76-63.

An easy win over Texas A&M Corpus Christi was followed by another difficult road trip, this time to Arizona. Arizona won 87-82. But the team came back to win its next five, including the Border War against Missouri at St. Louis. The record was a gaudy 11-2 going into the Big Ten season.

Here's where the roller-coaster ride got really scary.

On February 3, Illinois lost at home to Michigan State 67-61 to bring its conference record to 4-5. Fans are fickle, as we all know. They were down on Self, down on the team, down on each other, down on the announcers. This was rock bottom for a team that had been ranked by most as a top-three team in the United States.

I must admit that I took part in conversations around the water cooler about whether a 15-7, 4-5 team was good enough to make the NCAA tournament. It looked like the NIT to many of us.

Then a remarkable thing happened.

The Illini did a complete about-face. I credit Self and his staff with a marvelous piece of coaching during this time period. And I credit the members of the team for a gutsy, "us against the world" comeback.

Who would have dreamed that Illinois would not lose another conference game?

They ripped off seven straight conference wins, including four on the road, to finish 11-5 and 23-7 overall. A nonconference win at Seton Hall was mixed in with that fantastic finish. The Illini finished in a four-way tie for the conference championship, and Self became just the second coach in Big Ten history to win titles in his first two years of coaching in the league.

A win over Minnesota and a loss to Ohio State in the Big Ten conference tournament set the stage for yet another NCAA run. The Illini were seeded fourth and got a great site for the first round: the United Center in Chicago.

The year before Self came to Illinois, he led Tulsa to a 32-5 record and a berth in the Elite Eight. His first year at Illinois, his team got to the Elite Eight as well before losing to Arizona. He became the first coach to lead two different schools to the Elite eight back to back.

After beating San Diego State and Creighton to win yet another Sweet Sixteen appearance, the Illini lost to Kansas to finish the season 26-9.

Five seniors departed, but Self and his staff put together a highly ranked recruiting class, which included three from the state of Illinois and two from Texas. The future looks bright for Illinois basketball, and the biggest concern for Illinois fans now is how long Bill Self will stay.

Chapter 25

The Indiana Game

It was a helluva birthday party!

I turned seventy years old on February 26, 2002. That night at the Assembly Hall, I had the great honor and privilege of being on the court and handling the introduction of Illinois' five seniors, their parents, and friends. The opponent that night was Indiana: it was my final broadcast from the Assembly Hall. It was a night to remember and cherish.

The five seniors were in the process of completing a remarkable run that included two straight Big Ten cochampionships, three straight NCAA appearances, two trips to the Sweet Sixteen, one trip to the Elite Eight, an average 22.3 wins per season over the last four seasons, a 37-2 record at Assembly Hall over the past two seasons, and a 42-10 Assembly Hall record over the last four. They reached the semifinals of the Big Ten tournament all four years.

I remember the first time I met Cory Bradford. He and his grandparents were at the Assembly Hall on a recruiting visit. Lon Kruger told me where they were sitting, up in "B" section, behind the press section on the east side of the hall.

I walked up the stairs and introduced myself. Cory was sitting there, all hunched over, wearing a sweatshirt with a hood over his head. He shook my hand and mumbled something I couldn't understand. His grandfather was just the opposite.

He jumped up, smiling, shook my hand and said he was glad to meet me. We had a nice conversation, and I said I hoped they would consider Illinois, that it was a wonderful place to go to school and our basketball teams were terrific.

Cory did pick Illinois and had to sit out his freshman year as a partial qualifier. He would set what I consider to be one of the most remarkable records possible. He started every game of his collegiate career. He was there for the opening tip 134 straight times, a Big Ten record.

When others were sick and injured or benched for some reason, Cory was in the lineup. During his junior year, he hobbled on bad knees but never missed a start. During that same year, his consecutive three-pointer streak was stopped at eighty-eight–an NCAA record.

As I introduced Cory and his relatives the night of my birthday, I thought to myself how quickly time flies. It seemed only a short while ago that I had met him. The quiet, unassuming, hard-working young guy from Memphis will be difficult to replace. I, personally, will miss him.

Lucas Johnson didn't go out the way he wanted.

He tore his ACL in preseason and had surgery on October 22. This would be enough to keep most people off the court for a long, long time. But Lucas, tough guy that he is, returned just three months and one day after surgery. He wore a brace on the knee for the rest of the season and gutted it out, game after game.

Lucas will be remembered as a guy who did everything possible to help his team win. He dove for loose balls, took charges, scored crucial field goals, and harassed his men on defense. He was the kind of guy you would hate if he were on the other team, but as an Illini, he was one we loved and admired.

Lucas is the son of Ron and Leslie Johnson and the younger brother of Brian, who was a member of the Illini Big Ten championship team in 1998. Leslie came by the press box that night and thanked me for all the nice things I had said on the air about Lucas. I mentioned to her that she and Ron had been coming down to Champaign for Illini games for a long time.

"Yes," she said. "Nine years." I don't know how many games the Johnsons missed, at home and on the road, during the time their two sons played for Illinois, but I'm sure it wasn't many. What a wonderful family. It won't seem the same without them next year.

Damir Krupalija, like Lucas Johnson, was plagued by injuries during his senior year. He missed six games with a foot injury in December. He came back on January 23, played four games, reinjured the foot, and had surgery on February 6. He was finally able to return for the Big Ten tournament.

Damir was never fazed by adversity at Illinois. The problems he encountered here were nothing compared to what he faced earlier in his life. He fled war-torn Bosnia in 1992. After living in the Czech Republic for three years, he came to the United States, where he wound up playing at Rockford Boylan for Steve Goers. The Boylan teams were highly successful, finishing fourth in the state in 1997 and reaching the super sectional in 1996 and 1998.

During his senior year, Damir was named MVP of the Las Vegas tournament and seemed well on his way to a great final season when the foot injury occurred.

His parents, Sead and Zora, followed Damir's Illinois career very closely. I will always remember with great fondness the time spent with them before and after Illini games at the Assembly Hall.

Robert Archibald moved to the United States prior to his senior year in high school. He played one year at Lafayette High School in Ballwin, Missouri. His team finished second in the Class 3A tournament with a 30-2 record.

At Illinois, Archibald turned into a great defender and a high percentage shooter on the post. He will be very difficult to replace. One of his best games was the Elite Eight loss to Arizona his junior year when he scored twenty-five points. He also scored twenty-five against Penn State on February 20, 2002.

Robert was an easy guy to like. He was always very friendly and outgoing. He cracked me up when he said, "I'd like to welcome all of you to Jim Turpin Night," at the post-game press conference the night I was honored at the Assembly Hall on February 20.

Robert played most of his senior year with a bad back, but you'd never have known it, watching his 100 percent effort all the time. Bill Self's biggest chore in 2002-03 will be to find someone who can defend the post like Archibald did.

The fifth senior I introduced that night was Frank Williams.

I don't believe I have ever been around an Illinois player who received as much bad publicity as Frank did his senior year. It all started with CBS-TV's Billy Packer, who attacked Frank for his lack of effort on the court. He said Frank was "dogging it," or words to that effect. This caused Dick Vitale to join in a day or two later. Vitale agreed that Frank wasn't giving his all to the team. Writer after writer jumped on the "What's the matter with Frank Williams?" bandwagon.

Frank didn't help things much when he admitted that he didn't play all out all the time. "I pick my spots," he said.

This went on for several weeks during Frank's last season. If all the media nagging bothered him, he didn't show it. But it was certainly a distraction, and Bill Self grew weary of answering question after question about Frank. At one press conference, the always-amiable Self blurted out, "I am sick and tired of answering questions about Frank Williams." I wanted to applaud.

There is no doubt that Frank's style of play contributed to the controversy. His seemingly effortless way of handling the ball and blowing past defenders gave the appearance that he was only playing at half speed. He never yelled, never shook his fist in the air, never smiled very much, and never did all those motivational things that other point guards did.

Yet he was named Big Ten Player of the Year in 2001 by both coaches and the media. He was First Team All-Big Ten and Honorable Mention All-American in 2001 and 2002. He won game after game for the Illini with his last-minute heroics.

Frank surprised a lot of people when he came back for his senior year, when many felt he would opt for the NBA draft.

He came to Illinois as Mr. Basketball in the state of Illinois and was a McDonald's High School All-American. He was on Peoria Manual's state championship teams in 1995, 1996, and 1997.

I am hopeful that Frank Williams will be drafted and become a big star in the NBA. I believe that Frank's quiet demeanor on the court made him a misunderstood young man, especially during his senior year. It is difficult to know what motivates him. What I do know is that the Illinois basketball team would not have been nearly as successful during the past four years without Frank Williams. I will always remember him as a winner.

That night, after I walked off the court and began doing my last play-by-play in Assembly Hall, Illinois beat Indiana 70-62. Who could ask for more? What a birthday party!

Chapter 26

The Minnesota Game

By any measure, the Illini's last-second win over Minnesota on March 3, in the last game of the Big Ten's regular season, was unbelievable, unthinkable, and historical.

Consider these facts:

• Indiana, Ohio State, and Wisconsin had already clinched shares of the Big Ten championship with 11-5 records. The Illlini needed a victory at the Big Barn in Minneapolis to finish 11-5 and make it a four-way championship for the first time in seventy-five years of Big Ten competition.

• An Illinois win would give the team a third seed in the Big Ten tournament the following week and a bye for the opening round. An Illinois loss to Minnesota would mean the Illini would drop to a sixth seed and have to take part in an opening round "play-in" game.

• An Illinois win would mean that the Illini would earn their second straight conference title for the first time since the 1951 and 1952 seasons. Illinois had opened the Big Ten season 4-5, but then reeled off six straight conference wins heading into the Minnesota game.

• Illinois would register a rare feat with a victory: it would give the Illini Big Ten championships in both football and basketball in the same season. The last teams to do that at

Illinois were in 1983-84, when the football team went 9-0 and the basketball team went 15-3.

• A win over Minnesota would make Coach Bill Self the second Big Ten coach in history to win titles in each of his first two years, and the first since the 1912-14 seasons when Wisconsin's Walter Meanwell won titles in his first three years.

Not much at stake, right?

With all that riding on the line, Illinois did not play well early, committing turnover after turnover and getting down by as many as thirteen points in the first half. But they rallied and were down by just two at halftime.

The Illini actually took the lead for a short period in the second half, but Minnesota went back in front and the Golden Gophers appeared headed for another Big Barn victory. With thirty seconds to go, Minnesota was up four and had the ball. It looked like it was all over. I mean, it was *over*. But then—the miracle finish.

The Gophers led 66-62 when Frank Williams ripped the ball away from Kerwin Fleming of Minnesota. Williams grabbed the ball with both hands and, while falling backwards, flipped it to Cory Bradford. Bradford had one foot over the three-point line when he caught the ball, but he moved back behind the line and calmly sank the trey. The lead was now just one.

The Illini chose not to foul and again trapped the Gophers. This time Kevin Burleson threw the ball backwards, intending it for Dusty Rychart. Rychart was standing near the baseline, under the Illinois basket. But the pass was wide of Rychart and went out of bounds. Illinois ball!

Minnesota, which had been playing zone defense all day, went man to man against the out-of-bounds throw-in. Self ordered the ball thrown to Williams, who drove down the lane, split two defenders, and delivered a layup high off the board. The ball sank sweetly into the net with 2.9 seconds to go, and Illinois was up 67-66.

Minnesota tried a pass to near-center court, but the Gopher who grabbed it was out of bounds and the Illini had merely to inbound the ball. The pass went to Robert Archibald, who immediately threw the ball skyward. The game was over, and the Illini had won in one of the most exciting and improbable finishes I have ever seen. And they were Big Ten champs again!

A few hours later, despite bone-chilling cold, nearly 1,000 fans greeted the team at Willard Airport. The celebration was wild and wonderful. In many ways it was a dream-like experience. It's why people love college basketball. And this one was one for the books–truly unforgettable.

Chapter 27

Remembering Minnesota vs. Ohio State

Illinois' improbable come-from-behind victory at Minnesota on March 3 was one of the few times that the Illini left Williams Arena happy. This was one of the games that Illini fans will talk about for a long, long time.

The one game played at Williams Arena that I remember the most did not involve the Illini. It was played on January 25, 1972. Ohio State came to town leading the Big Ten with a 3-0 record. What happened that night was one of the saddest and most shocking incidents in the history of Big Ten basketball.

The Buckeyes were riding high under Coach Fred Taylor. They had won the conference title the year before, and it was their seventh title in twelve years. They had been to the Final Four in 1968, their fourth trip in nine years.

But when the night was over, the game of basketball was never quite the same for several Buckeye players. Even Minnesota fans were quoted as saying they never wanted to see another basketball game after what happened.

Columbus sports columnist Bob Hunter wrote:

"However you see the events that transpired in Williams Arena, there is no denying that the OSU basketball program has never again reached the heights it achieved before that fateful night in Minnesota, the night that several Gopher players and fans took out their desperation in losing on the unsuspecting visitors from Ohio State."

Bill Musselman, the Gophers' young coach, hailed the matchup as the biggest game in Minnesota basketball history, one the Gophers simply had to win to make their program great."

Luke Witte, Ohio State's center, drove in for a layup with thirty-six seconds remaining in the game and the Buckeyes on top 50-44. He ran into Gophers Corky Taylor and Clyde Turner. Witte went down. Taylor reached down and stuck out his hand. It appeared that he was going to help Witte up, but when Witte reached up to grab Taylor's hand, Taylor kneed him in the groin. All hell broke loose.

Ron Behagen, another Gopher player, ran onto the court from the bench and kicked Witte in the head. Some Minnesota fans charged onto the court and began slugging OSU players. Three Buckeyes–Witte, Mark Wager, and Mark Minor–wound up in the hospital. Both Witte and Wager had concussions. Minor had cuts and abrasions.

Ohio State's Coach Taylor was quoted after the game:

"I went up and picked Behagen up off Witte and held him in the air. He was screaming like an animal. Finally, I look around and it looks like things are quieting down, and he is screaming for me to put him down, so I put him down and he went running about seventy-five feet down the court and aimed a flying kick at Dave Merchant's crotch. Dave saw it coming and got a little bit out of the way, but the kick hit him in the thigh, and Dave's leg was black and blue all the way down to the ankle. If he had hit him in the crotch, it would have killed him."

Hunter wrote, "The incident had a profound effect on Taylor and his team. Taylor felt OSU athletic director Ed Weaver didn't push hard enough for the Gophers to be punished. Taylor became embittered after the Gophers beat OSU in a return match in Columbus and Weaver was just happy no incidents occurred."

Minnesota won the Big Ten title. The Buckeyes were invited to the NIT, but voted not to go. They had enough of basketball.

Witte said, "I didn't want to play anymore. I don't think I can say even now that I regret the decision because of how I felt about basketball at the time."

Most of the players felt the same way. The next season OSU finished 14-10. In the years after, the team went 9-15, 14-14, and 6-20. Taylor lost interest in coaching and recruiting after the incident and quit his job in 1976. He died in 2002.

Hunter concluded, "The program has been all over the map since then, approaching the heights of the Taylor days with Jim Jackson, but never quite regaining the status it held under Taylor. Would all have been different if there had been no mugging? Twenty-five years later, it is still easy to wonder what might have been."

Every time I go to Williams Arena, I think about that night, that game, that beating that the OSU players took from Minnesota players and fans.

The current Ohio State players weren't even born when the incident took place. This year, the Buckeyes tied for the Big Ten title and won the conference tournament before bowing out to Missouri in the NCAA tournament.

I wonder how many of them even know about the Minnesota incident? I agree with Taylor when he said it was the sorriest incident he'd ever seen in intercollegiate athletics.

Chapter 28

The Big Dance

It is my opinion that the greatest of all sporting events is the NCAA Men's Basketball Tournament–the Big Dance!

The World Series, the Super Bowl, the Stanley Cup, bowl games, the Davis Cup, the Indy 500, NASCAR races–I love 'em all because I'm a sports nut, but none compares to the Big Dance.

Teams go 30-0, teams win conference championships, teams win conference tournaments, teams win the big tournaments, and teams set all kinds of personal and team records, but they are remembered by how they did in the Big Dance.

Does anyone, other than staunch Hoosier fans, remember how many total games Indiana won last year, or how many conference games they won, or how they did in the Big Ten conference tournament? Probably not. But basketball fans everywhere remember the great run Mike Davis's team made in the Big Dance, finishing second in the nation to champion Maryland.

Thus the fondest basketball memory Illinois fans have is 1989, when the Flying Illini got to the Final Four only to lose to hated Michigan, a team they had beaten twice before during the regular season. The Flying Illini won thirty-one games that year and earned a No. 1 seed in the Big Dance. It seems like only yesterday that the Flying Illini knocked off

McNeese State, Ball State, Louisville, and Syracuse. It seems like only yesterday because it happened in the Big Dance.

Bill Self's first two teams at Illinois won back to back Big Ten championships. They won twenty-seven games the first year and twenty-six the second year. But I'll bet you that in years to come, Illini fans will talk about the two games against Kansas in the Big Dance–a win the first year and a loss the second year. That's just the way it is.

Fans by the millions sit glued to the TV set on selection Sunday. "Will we get in? What kind of seed will we get? Where will we play? Who will we play? Who else is in our bracket?"

Immediately, brackets are printed and filled out. Not just by basketball fans, but also by people who don't know Duke from Delaware. Oftentimes someone who picked Maryland because his or her daughter is named Marilyn wins office pools.

Then in that first round, when the Zags are upset by the Zigs and the higher-seeded teams tumble to lower-seeded ones, "My bracket is shot. I had them going to the Final Four and they lose in the first round!"

The joy of it all.

The 2001-2002 Illini drew a No. 4 seed. They had hoped for a three. But they were sent to the United Center in Chicago where they had played many other games–a definite plus. Win two games there and it's on to Madison, Wisconsin, and the Kohl Center.

The Illini drew the No. 13 seed, San Diego State, in the first round. A win against the Aztecs would probably throw Illinois into a second-round game against the fifth-seeded Florida Gators.

But Billy Donovan's team didn't make it past the first round, losing to Creighton 83-82. The Illini had little trouble with San Diego State, winning 93-64.

That set up a second-round game of Illinois vs. Creighton. It was on to Madison and the round of sixteen for the winner.

Frank Williams scored all twenty of his points in the second half against Creighton with Brian Cook adding sixteen, Cory Bradford twelve, and Robert Archibald eleven, as the Illini won 72-60.

Meanwhile, the number-one seed in the Midwest Regional, the Kansas Jayhawks, had advanced to the Sweet Sixteen with wins over Holy Cross and Stanford, setting up another Kansas-Illinois matchup. The previous year, Illinois had beaten Kansas to advance to the Elite Eight.

As we walked up the sidewalk leading to the entrance of the Kohl Center prior to the Illinois-Kansas game, a group of about forty protesters with "Racist Mascot" signs were demonstrating. Obviously, the signs were aimed at Chief Illiniwek. I think I stunned them when I walked up close and said, "I didn't know a Jayhawk was a racist mascot." The young woman I had spoken to opened her mouth to say something back, but nothing came out. I hurried on into the building, content with my small victory.

But there would be no victory that night for Illinois, small or large. A talented Kansas team won a hard-fought, down-to-the-wire game in which Illinois had shots to take the lead or tie in the final minutes, but couldn't connect. Two days later Kansas beat Oregon and advanced to the Final Four.

I signed off the broadcast as usual:

"I'm Jim Turpin. Goodbye for now."

After forty years, it was my last Illini broadcast.

Chapter 29

Honors Banquet

I have had the great pleasure of attending dozens of banquets honoring athletes in all sports during my career. I have been the master of ceremonies at many of them, including football and men's basketball.

Some are great; some are not so great. In fact, some have been downright boring, no doubt the fault of the bumbling MC, long-winded speeches, poor food service, poor food, and a tendency to forget that the kids are the ones being honored and that they should be permitted to share the podium.

The biggest problem banquet planners have is trying to jam too much into the program, and it drags on and on. Have you ever heard anyone leave a banquet and say, "Gee, that was too short?" More likely, it's, "What time is it? Let's get out of here."

One of the best, if not *the* best, banquets I've ever been associated with happened in 2002. It was the 80th Annual Fighting Illini Men's Basketball Banquet, held on April 9 at the Round Barn Center in Champaign. More than 600 people jammed into the hall, and they were thoroughly entertained. Frankly, I never heard one complaint.

This banquet had everything: a great highlights video, some funny stuff, some sad stuff, plenty of emotion, and another Bill Self performance that had the audience crying and laughing. Even the MC got a little emotional, and so did the coach. But the acceptance of the awards and the comments of the departing seniors were the most memorable moments.

Here are some of the comments from the coach and the players. Bill Self began.

"As you know, we had really good players this year. As you also know, they are better people than they are players. This was, arguably, the most rewarding, gratifying, toughest and frustrating year that I have ever coached. And for the fans, it may have been the same with you as far as cheering and everything. I will say this: it could not have been scripted better for these guys (seniors) to leave out of here, taking this with them, because they know now that when the chips are down, they have got it inside them to fight back. And that's what life is all about.

"We were preseason picks to win the Big Ten conference title. We were picked that way with a healthy Damir and a healthy Lucas. We go to Missouri and beat an Elite Eight team with Damir playing on one foot, with Archibald, who hadn't practiced in a week, and Lucas not healthy. That was a remarkable feat.

"Then we start out 4-5 in the league and there was a lot of criticism, much of it deserved, very much deserved, but these guys fought and hung together.

"The thing that really impresses me most when you look at all these seniors–and you are only as good as your seniors allow you to be–you have Cory who played all last year on one leg; Damir missed about a season's worth of games during his career, but he had the attitude to come back, come back, come back and gave us a chance to win. Do you realize that we had no chance to win the Big Ten championship if he didn't come back? Look at Lucas. He's the only guy I know who would have his car spray-painted orange and think it was cool. Lucas tore up his knee and the trainer and doctors did a great job but in two and a half months he was back playing. That doesn't happen!

"That doesn't happen unless you want it really, really bad.

"And then you have Arch. Arch had one of the better gigs in college basketball–play a day, take a day off. Arch, it's not like that in the real world. You're going to have to go to work more than three days a week. But the guy had a great year. He had a bad back; he had a bad hand; he had a bad something all the time. But when it was time to play, the guy competed!

"And that brings us to the last senior. Frank is probably the toughest kid I have ever coached. I have never seen anybody take the heat that Frank took, undeservedly, this year. Now, there were times when Frank brought a little bit of it on himself. But the guy is a warrior. And think about it, when it got the hottest, he was taking the heat for everybody else. When we weren't making shots, it came back to Frank. When we weren't guarding or rebounding, it came back to Frank. And never once, no matter what the situation was, did these guys ever point a finger. They stuck together, and they gave us a chance."

Self then recognized other members of the team.

"In order to win, you have to recruit men with character, and not characters. We've been very fortunate to recruit these kinds of men in our program. And you look around this room, and you see the families. The five sets of parents that we are going to be losing are going to be missed, too. These are really good people that sent really good sons to be ambassadors for this university. We appreciate that.

"Luther Head has an unbelievable amount of ability. He probably had to go to the bathroom when Ron Guenther said we might be playing in front of 30,000 people down in St. Louis. The crowds at Manley High School weren't quite that big, were they, Coach Delaney? You were a good player at Manley, but now we know why you got to play so much. The coach married your mother, right?

"Roger Powell may be as physically tough as anyone on our team. We had to play him out of position this year. He's a guy that probably led the nation in shots per minute.

"Nick Smith has great potential. He has great hands. He's a great shooter. He has bulked up from 222 to 225. I think he's going to be a tremendous basketball player.

"Brett Melton is going to be a tremendous player for us. He is working on re-habbing his ankle. We hope it is just a formality that he gets his red-shirt year. You'll see a lot of him next year. He can really shoot the rock.

"Jerrance Howard hasn't played much yet because we have had some veteran guys ahead of him, but he will play. He is one of the most fun kids I've ever been around. He's a tremendous recruiter. He represents the school well. And he busts his tail every day in practice.

"Nick Huge isn't very well known yet. Nick will be eligible next year. He is a transfer from Appalachian State. You'll see more of him next year.

"Clayton Thomas gets beat up every day in practice and very rarely does he fight back because we don't want him to hurt any of the guys who are going to play more. Clayton, your hair is almost back to its original color. Looks good!

"Blandon Ferguson is a JC transfer. It took him a while to get adjusted. And to get used to me. That's not always easy to do. He'll be the first to tell you. He has great athletic ability, and he'll really help us next year. You can tell he's from California and a little soft. It's 70 degrees outside, and he's wearing a turtleneck all the way up. He thinks it's cold here.

"Sean Harrington is a guy who has made a lot of big shots for us the two years I've been here. We were able to recruit him out of the Chicago area. I think he is a guy that is getting ready to step into a leadership role and become more vocal. If Sean looks a little bit different, it's because Arch has been working with him on his hair.

"Brian Cook is going to be one of the best, if not *the* best, senior in America next year. His confidence level has shot off the charts. He is a tremendous, tremendous player, and it is going to be interesting for him to take on the role of a leader and be the focal point of the team, which I think he is really excited about."

Then, Coach Self began to talk about his seniors:

"Damir Krupalija is a tough guy. And I'll tell you what, a lot of women in the stands are heartbroken tonight because Damir is graduating. He is obviously a class guy. He speaks about fourteen different languages, and I think he has cussed at me in twelve of them. He's a guy who has a chance to continue to play either here or overseas and make some good money.

"The next senior is a guy who you expect the unexpected with. It's remarkable to me to have known him for two years now and all of a sudden he wears glasses to try to look smarter. You'll get a job, Lucas; don't worry about it. But he's tough, he's ornery, he's the kind of player you love if he is on your team. If he's on the other team, you may love to hate him a little bit. Bottom line: we got no chance to win the Big Ten championship this year unless he busts his butt and gets back early. No chance.

"He made some great plays, playing at about 80 percent. I don't think he has any regrets, because he has himself two rings. Lucas Johnson.

"The next senior is tough. He could be a Marlboro commercial. He's from Scotland. When we came here, we thought Robert would be a good player, but he has become someone that I believe will be a draft pick and who knows what will happen after that. He plays in pain, does what he is supposed to do, and loves to compete. Arch would like to leave Illinois knowing that he does have the best hair in college basketball. Robert Archibald.

"The next senior is obviously a highly, highly touted guy from Peoria. This guy is as talented as any player that I have ever been around. I don't know if a guy could have gone to a better place to prepare him for what's ahead than Illinois. Frank has gone through some good times and some bad times. And trust me, Frank, when you are in Boston or New York next year, there will be some fans who'll treat you good and some who'll treat you bad. The thing that I think I'll miss most about Frank is his imagination. He has the best imagination on the court of anybody I have ever coached. When he screwed up, I very rarely ever took him out because he would come to the bench and say, 'Coach, you didn't see that?' I trusted him that he was always telling me the truth. He's obviously a major talent. He was Big Ten Player of the Year last year and, in my opinion, he had a bad three-week stretch or he would have been Big Ten Player of the Year again this year. That's Frank Williams.

"No one represents the University of Illinois and Illini basketball better than Cory Bradford. Cory is tough. He came in as a two-guard. They made him a one-guard and he led the team in scoring. I've been reminded a lot that before I came here Cory scored a lot. You talk about a fun guy to coach. He plays hurt. Does the dirty work. Sacrifices for the good of others. These seniors are all going to graduate this May. Frank has a little more to do since he is leaving early. A winner in every right, Cory Bradford."

Then came the awards.

The first award was the Ralf Woods Free Throw trophy, which went to junior Brian Cook who shot at 89 percent. Cook was a repeat winner of the award.

Then two awards were presented, and the emotions burst all over the big hall.

The first was the Kenny Battle Award, named after the young man who was the heart of the 1989 Illini Final Four team. The award goes to the player his teammates deem as most inspirational. Cory Bradford was surprised when Bill Self named him the winner. He said, "I wasn't expecting to get this. I expected Lucas Johnson to get it." Cory stopped speaking and began crying. "Lucas, can you come up?" They hugged and the audience applauded.

"We all know this award goes to you, man," Cory said, still crying. "You could have given up on us, but you didn't. I love you for that. I appreciate everything you have done for us. From last place our freshman year. To two Big Ten championships. By far, you have been the heart and soul of our team. And, we always fed off you. This award should go to you. I thank you for everything, brother."

Then, Lucas broke in with a lighter comment: "And he still goes home with the trophy."

The Matto Award followed. The award was named after Matt Heldman, who led the Illini to the Big Ten championship in 1997. Matt and his father were killed in an automobile accident a few years ago. The award goes to the player who showed the greatest hustle during the year. It went to Lucas Johnson.

"First and foremost I want to thank our Lord above," Lucas said. "He is the reason I was able to come back this year. I want to thank my parents. You guys have probably never seen a mom more on TV than my mom. Or a mom who watched the game less. They have been here for me for four years. It has been tough this year. I hurt my knee, and I wanted to play with these guys so bad. With lots of support from my parents, my friends, and my teammates, I was able to come back. I wouldn't have traded it for the world. I'm going to miss the guys on this team, especially these seniors.

"I'm going to miss them like they are my brothers. I do what I do to help us win; it is not for personal glory. No one does what I do for personal glory. I am most honored not because the plaque has my name on it, but because it has Matt's. I knew him personally. I miss him like a brother. He was an inspiration to me, and he should be an inspiration to a lot more people. Thank you very much."

Then Coach Self asked the other seniors to address the crowd. First was Damir.

"I think everybody has had about enough of crying, so I'll make this short and sweet. These guys mean a lot to me. We are glad we were able to do what we did the past four years. Hopefully, you guys coming back can win the big trophy."

Robert Archibald continued.

"During the past few years we had as much fun as you can have playing basketball, and we worked as hard as any team. That's a rare combination. We seniors all came from different backgrounds and all with different personalities. But you throw us all together now, and it looks like we grew up together on the same street and hung out with each other every day. To my parents, everything I have been able to do here has been a direct reflection on everything you have given me a chance to do. Thank you."

The final award–MVP–went to Frank Williams.

"My years here have been great. The guys around me have really supported me through the tough times that I had. I wouldn't have wanted to be around any other group. I'd like to let my mom know how much I love her. She raised a lot of kids, a lot of us, and she had a rough time doing that. I will always remember where I came from. This is the place I would like for my son to come to."

A final comment came from Bill Self.

"No matter who this university ever recruits in the future, they're not going to recruit five better citizens than those who are leaving us. They have made our job fun. I wouldn't trade anything, not the good times, not the bad times. The highs far exceeded the lows, and a coach couldn't have been any happier than when Frank made that shot to beat Minnesota."

Thus ended the 2002 Men's Basketball Banquet.

I wish you could all have been there. It was very, very special.

Chapter 30

Basketball Blues

For me personally, the 2001-02 basketball season proved very difficult to handle. A mysterious physical ailment caused me to miss several games and to suffer through many others. It took some of the fun out of it, for sure.

Physicians at Carle Clinic in Urbana treated me for several months prior to deciding that my problem was interstitial cystitis. IC is a chronic inflammation of the bladder wall. Its cause is unknown, and there is no cure.

Common cystitis is a urinary tract infection caused by bacteria and is usually successfully treated with antibiotics. IC is believed not to be caused by bacteria and does not respond to conventional antibiotic therapy. IC is not a psychosomatic disorder, nor is it caused by stress.

IC can affect people of any age, race, or sex. It is, however, most commonly found in women. It is almost never found in 70-year-old men. I always like to be the exception–unique and different! (Right!)

The symptoms of IC are frequency of urination, urgency, and extreme pain in the abdominal or urethral areas.

The simple explanation is: you have to go to the potty quickly, often, and it hurts when you do. Riding on a bus, flying in an airplane, walking up stairs, and sitting in the same position for long periods of time are the hardest activities to cope with.

Thus, I had no choice but to miss some road games, which I hated to do, especially during my last season. But it could not be helped. Thanks to my colleagues for being so understanding and so helpful in getting me through this difficult period.

These sudden trips to the restroom caused some interesting things to happen:

In the old field house at Wisconsin our broadcast area was in the top row of the balcony. Fans were jammed in tightly with their knees in our backs. The only restroom was at floor level. At halftime I fought my way through the crowd and down the long flights of stairs to the restroom area where a long, long line awaited me. I stood in line for several minutes, but it was plain to see on this night that I wasn't going to get back upstairs in time for the second half to start. So I made a quick decision: I opened the door and stepped outside into a bitterly cold, snowy night in Madison. Luckily no one else was out there. Only after I finished my business did I think about the possibility of the next day's headline: "Illini Play-by-Play Announcer Arrested For Indecent Exposure."

Another time, at the United Center, I simply could not make it until halftime, so I turned quickly to Brian Barnhart and he took over the play-by-play. An announcer on "The Score" was at the game, saw me leave, and actually reported it on the air during his postgame show. He called it "unprofessional." I heard him say that as I was driving home and listening to his show. It was hurtful to hear. I was tempted to call or write a letter or something, but resisted. I'm telling him now, "Buster, you are the one who is unprofessional. I hope you never have I.C." Then again.......

Section 4

THE GUYS

Chapter 31

The Players

O ne of the most frequent questions people ask me is "Who were your favorite players?" That is an entirely different question than, "Who were your favorite people?" There is a big, big difference in admiring a player's ability on the playing field and admiring him as an individual.

Players come in all shapes and sizes and have such diverse personalities that you wonder if they all came from the same planet. In other words, they are just like you and me and our friends and neighbors.

To me, the hardest part is watching what has happened to some players and people that I have known during my career who have let their lives get away from them. It is so sad, but in most cases they have no one to blame but themselves. I believe strongly in personal responsibility and not blaming others for your mistakes and shortcomings.

Case in point: Ervin Small.

Ervin came to Illinois with Nick Anderson from Chicago's Simeon High School. Many felt that Ervin was just a throw-in and would not play a very significant role for Lou Henson's basketball team. Nick was the guy; Ervin was just along for the ride. To a certain extent, that turned out to be right. Nick became one of Illinois' greatest players, leading the Illini to the Final Four in 1989 and then embarking on a distinguished career in the NBA. But Ervin did his share. He became a very valuable backup player and made some wonderful contributions to that '89 team.

In addition to making contributions on the court, Ervin was a delight to be around off the court. He was always smiling. He played a big role in developing the famous rap songs that the '89 team sang. Many of the hysterical lyrics, aimed at each Illini and Coach Lou, were penned by Ervin and Kenny Battle. Every time I'd see Ervin he would flash that big smile, give me a high five, and ask how I'm doin' and how's my wife doin'; "Tell her I said hello," he'd say, and he was so sweet and so sincere I knew he meant every word of it.

My wife, Louise, and I were invited to Ervin's wedding. It was a giant bash held in Champaign. It started about an hour late, but it made up for it on the other end; I don't know when that thing got over. I have a photograph from that wedding which hung in my office for years. It was a photo of Ervin and his wife, best man Jimmy Collins, and groomsmen Nick Anderson, Steve Bardo, Kendall Gill, Marcus Liberty, Kenny Battle, and Andy Kpedi.

Ervin had always wanted to become involved in law enforcement, so it was no surprise that following graduation he was hired as a prison guard at the Danville Correctional Facility.

What happened next was a heartbreaker. Ervin was arrested for selling drugs and was sent to prison. I went to see him while he was being held at the DeWitt County facility in Clinton, awaiting sentencing. As I entered the visitor's area, separated from the prisoners by a glass wall, Ervin saw me and began to smile.

We began to chat about what was happening in my life, and then I asked him how he was doing. The big smile disappeared. Then he began to cry. I didn't know what to do or what to say. "Mr. Jim, I really screwed up," he said. "I really screwed up." He looked down. He seemed very sad and embarrassed. I tried to console him and say a few upbeat things, but I know I was totally inadequate. I felt sorry for him. He looked so young, so fragile, and so vulnerable, not at all like the tough kid who took on Nervous Pervis Ellison in the Illinois-Louisville game in '89.

About that time his wife and child, who had come to visit, entered the room. I said hello to them and said I needed to be on my way anyway, so they could visit in privacy. It was really an escape. I needed to get out of there. As I was leaving, Ervin put his big hand on the glass and I did the same on the other side. It was a poor excuse for a high five, but the best we could do under the circumstances. He thanked me for coming. I said something really inane, something like "keep your head up" or "hang in there." Then I left. That is the last time I saw Ervin Small. But when anyone asks about my favorite players among all those I have covered as a play-by-play man, he is one that I think of.

He made a big mistake. As he said, "I really screwed up."

I think also of Larry Smith, a member of the Final Four team, and Rennie Clemons, a kid from Springfield who had so much promise. They, too, screwed up. Then there's Mark Smith, a young guy with a world of talent. He played on the same Illini team as Eddie Johnson. Mark Smith died last year. Eddie Johnson, like Nick Anderson, had a long and distinguished NBA career.

Speaking of Anderson, I will never forget what he said repeatedly the night we came back from Seattle after losing to Michigan in the Final Four. Thousands of fans had gathered in the Assembly Hall to greet the team. A stage had been erected at center court and a "yellow brick road" had been constructed leading from the tunnel to the stage. I had the great pleasure of being the MC that night, so I was in the tunnel with the team, the Hensons and the other coaches, plus other university officials. As we waited for the signal to proceed to the stage, Anderson and I talked. We had always had a great relationship, and I was really quite fond of him. I still am.

"They're going to want to know if you're coming back next year," I told him.

"I know. I am coming back. No doubt about it. I'll be back," he replied.

As the season wound down and Nick continued to play in a spectacular fashion, the rumors were flying that he would turn pro and give up his last year of eligibility. Remember, this was 1989, and turning pro didn't happen as often as it does now, when dozens of collegiate underclassmen and high school stars declare for the NBA draft every year.

A few minutes later, when all the participants had followed the yellow brick road to the stage amid a thunderous ovation, I grabbed the mic and said something like, "We're here tonight to honor the best basketball team in Illinois history!!" The roar from the crowd was deafening. They agreed.

After university officials spoke, the team was introduced one by one and each gave a little talk. I remember distinctly that the ovation for Anderson was the longest and the loudest. Nick, in his own shy way, said thanks to everyone for their support and finished his talk with, "And I'll be back next year!" The crowd went crazy. That's what they had wanted to hear. I sincerely believe that Nick felt in his own heart, at that moment, that he would be back.

As all Illini fans know, it didn't happen. Agents and Nick's pro friends got to him and described the amount of money he would make that next year as an NBA player. Nick's mother had been injured in an automobile accident and was unable to go back to work. Nick felt that he needed to support her and the rest of his family (a sister and two brothers) and that he had no choice but to turn pro and take the money.

His coach, Lou Henson, didn't try to talk Nick out of the decision, but said only that he thought Nick would be a higher draft pick the next year and would make even more money. The Orlando Magic, an expansion team, picked Nick eleventh in the draft. He spent several productive years there and was loved by Magic fans, just as he was by the Illini faithful.

Years went by and Nick never returned to the campus. Close friends of his said he was afraid to come back, afraid that people were mad at him. He just didn't want to face them. Just last year, the Final Four team held a reunion and played a fun game against some former Illini football players at the Assembly Hall. At a reception prior to the game I walked up to Nick, and we hugged. I cried a little, and so did he. There were a lot of hugs and a lot of tears that night. And when the players were introduced at the game, the loudest cheers were for Nick Anderson.

I can still see that shot at Indiana, and I can still see him shooting that little jumper and bulling his way in there for a rebound. I can still remember him willing the Illini to victory after victory. He had a combination of sweetness and toughness—a rarity. There have been some great players at Illinois, and I have seen a lot of them in person. Was he the best? It is impossible to rank them, but it is easy to say that he would be in the top three.

I admired and respected Derek Harper as a player and a person, but he disappointed me during his final days at Illinois. What he did was hurtful and totally unnecessary. After he left Illinois and became an NBA standout, I still followed his box scores, and Loren Tate and I would have him on "Saturday Sportsline." But despite my efforts to forgive and forget, my memories of Derek are still clouded by his inconsiderate actions during a time when I was trying to be his friend.

Harper was generally considered to be the best high school guard in the nation in 1980. He was being recruited out of West Palm Beach, Florida, by dozens of universities. When he wound up at Illinois, after some masterful and persistent recruiting by Illini assistant Tony Yates, Harper was considered the biggest catch ever. Illini fans couldn't believe that Illinois beat Michigan, Florida, Florida State, and others for Harper's services.

In my opinion, he proved to be one of the top three best players ever to wear the orange and blue. He had the quickest hands I've ever seen. Bruce Douglas was quick, but Harper was quicker. When he left school, he was Illinois' all-time leader in assists and steals. He was simply a joy to watch.

Derek and I became friends during his time at Illinois. Not all players are anxious to befriend members of the media. Many are distrustful of writers and broadcasters, sometimes with good reason. But Derek was different, at least to me. He was always open, was a great interview, and we had a lot of nonbasketball talks, especially on road trips. He was not just another player. He was a friend.

Thus it was quite a shock and surprise the way he responded to my efforts to help and befriend him during a difficult time in his life.

Harper had three great years at Illinois, and when it came time for players to declare for the NBA draft prior to his senior year, rumors began to fly that Derek was going to turn pro. Would he or wouldn't he? One day he was going, the next day he was staying. To complicate matters, Lou Henson was taking his team on a trip to Yugoslavia during the off season, and no one knew if Harper was going or not. If he went on that trip it would be an indication that he intended to play his senior year at Illinois. If he passed on the trip, it would be the end of his Illinois career, and he would be headed for the NBA.

Several of us showed up at Willard Airport on the day the team was to leave. We wanted to wish them well, but mostly we wanted to see if Harper would get on the plane with his teammates. Rod Cardinal, the Illini trainer and trip coordinator, had Harper's equipment bags brought to the airport, just in case.

Harper had reportedly told people that he was going with the team and would be at the airport that morning. Departure time came, and there was no Derek.

As I drove home from the airport, disappointed at the outcome, I began to think that Derek was probably sitting at home, lonely and confused. I decided to call him up. He answered the phone, and I asked if he wanted some company. He said, "Sure, come on over."

When I arrived at his Urbana apartment, his roommate answered the door and said Derek was not there. I said I had just talked to him moments ago, and that he had invited me over. The roommate said he didn't know where Derek was. He thought perhaps he had gone out to shoot some baskets. I had the strangest feeling that Derek was hiding out in the bedroom. So I left.

Later in the day, I felt I just had to talk to him. So I called him again. Again, he answered the phone. I said my wife and I would like to have him over for dinner that night, just to talk and relax. He said that sounded great and asked what time he should come. We said about six o'clock would be great. He said he would be there, and he deeply appreciated the invitation and our concern for his welfare during these troubled times.

My wife fixed a nice dinner, and we waited. And waited, and waited. At seven-thirty I called his apartment. There was no answer. We ate dinner by ourselves wondering all the while what had happened to friendship, reliability, and good manners.

We learned later that Derek had sent his letter to the NBA a few days earlier, and he never intended to make the trip to Yugoslavia. He had kept us all hanging for no good reason. No one resented him going pro. He had ten brothers and sisters and a single mom, and he had the opportunity to make a lot of money.

All he had to do was say, "I'm going." That would have been the end of it.

I'm proud of Derek's accomplishments, and by all accounts he has been a model citizen as an NBA player, which is more than can be said for so many of them.

But even now, when I see his name mentioned, I think back to that bizarre day when he avoided my wife and me when we just wanted to befriend him.

Chapter 32

More Players

Matt Heldman had a funny-looking jump shot. Matt Heldman was the ultimate leader of a championship team.

Matt Heldman was fun to be around. He liked jokes. His teammates had fun pulling jokes on him.

Matt Heldman was as courteous and nice as any Illini player I've ever been around. He always smiled and said hello and appeared to be genuinely interested in what an old announcer had to say.

Matt Heldman died much too soon.

When the 1997-98 season began, no one picked Illinois to finish in the first division of the Big Ten, much less share in the championship. The starters were all seniors, but there were big question marks, not the least of which was who would play the point. Who would lead this team?

The Illini were hoping that Robbie Reid, a transfer from BYU, would be the guy, but he chose Michigan instead. Heldman had been a starter the previous year in a three-guard lineup that included Kiwane Garris and Kevin Turner. Garris was one of the best point guards ever at Illinois. Now someone else needed to step up.

That guy was Matt Heldman.

His play in early games convinced second-year coach Lon Kruger that Heldman could handle the point. His clutch free-throw shooting and his ability to hit that funny-looking jumper in crucial situations helped Illinois to a 23-10 record overall and l3-3 in the Big Ten. Major roles were played by Jarrod Gee, Jerry Hester, Brian Johnson, and Kevin Turner, the other four seniors, but there is no doubt that there would have been no championship without Matt Heldman. I loved to watch him play. Matt was another example of a too-small and too-slow kid who turned out to be a champion because of hard work, desire, and a personality that made you want to go hug him all the time!

Matt and his father, Otis, were killed on October 10, 1999, in a car wreck just outside his hometown of Libertyville. Two other people also died in the two-car crash.

Gene Cross is my kind of guy.

Cross came to the University of Illinois from Olympia Fields. He had played at Rich Central. He won letters in 1993 and 1994 and was a member of teams that included more familiar names: Tom Michael, Deon Thomas, T.J. Wheeler, Kiwane Garris, Richard Keene, Shelly Clark, Andy Kaufmann, and Rennie Clemons.

Lou Henson decided that he would take his team on an international trip and was convinced by someone that a good time could be had by all if the Illini visited Russia, Latvia, and Lithuania. He invited my wife and me to accompany the team, along with several other boosters and friends of the Illini. Gene Cross was on that trip.

I don't want to intimate that my wife had a difficult time choosing what to take on such a trip, but her suitcase was bulging and it was heavy! At some point during the early part of the trip she was struggling, as we all were, to carry our luggage from place to place. This was not exactly a Class A Prime Time Trip; there were no bellhops, no red-caps, nobody to assist.

"Mrs. Turpin, let me help you with that," said Gene Cross. He grabbed her suitcase and off he went. And it didn't happen just once. He carried that heavy load for Louise virtually every day that we were on the move.

It's strange what you remember. I forget who we played (except for the Lithuanian National Team) and what the scores were. We did a lot of sightseeing, but I have forgotten much of what we saw. We did have a wild train ride one night that is best remembered for its crowded conditions and its smelly toilets.

What I do remember is one young gentleman who was never a star player at Illinois, who never made the headlines, but who was kind enough and thoughtful enough to assist my wife.

I have seen Gene Cross several times since then. He has always been extremely friendly, and we've had some good basketball chats. I don't know that I ever properly thanked him for his kindness, so I am doing it now.

Gene is now an assistant basketball coach at DePaul.

Chapter 33

Jean Driscoll

Illinois Power is not needed when Jean Driscoll enters the room. She lights it up all by herself. That smile. Those eyes. The confidence and self-assuredness that only a few people have–those who know where they have been, where they are going, and how they are going to get there.

You don't become an accomplished speaker, singer, and songwriter by just wishing it would happen. You don't become the greatest wheelchair racer in history by just thinking about it. And you don't emerge from a long stint in a full-body cast to become one of sports' most admired women unless you have guts, discipline, and dedication.

Jean Driscoll's rise to international prominence, including her incredible eight victories in the Boston Marathon, is well known in Illini land. In fact, she has a book that tells all about it.

My wife and I have gotten to know Jean personally during my broadcast days at Illinois, and there is no doubt that she would rank very near the top of my "Most Admired Illini" list.

Jean loves to tell the story about being hospitalized and the nurse who was going to give her a shot.

"She asked me to roll up my sleeve and she looked at my upper arm and biceps. She said, 'Goodness, my dear, your arm is all swollen.' Then she looked at my other arm and said, 'This one is, too.' Apparently she had not seen the arms of a wheelchair racer before. My arms weren't swollen. It was the muscles that I had developed after all those miles on the road and all those hours in the weight room. I thought it was very funny."

Over dinner one night at Biaggi's restaurant in Champaign, Jean told Louise and me about her love of God, how He gave her the strength and guidance needed to overcome her physical problems and how He enabled her to achieve such an amazing record in wheelchair racing.

Later that evening Jean was eager to show us the new house that she had just purchased. Inside, we were able to see just some of the Olympic and Boston medals that she had on display. It was mind-blowing.

Louise went back to the house a few days after that and planted some flowers for Jean, and she was so appreciative. She likes to work in her garden, and she said, "I just love to shovel snow."

It is fun to watch her get into her van, leaping from her wheelchair into the driver's seat, then reaching down, grabbing the wheelchair and literally flinging it into the back seat. It's those "swollen" arms at work again.

I have heard Jean speak to large audiences, such as the Fellowship of Christian Athletes and Developmental Services Center, and she really does a wonderful job. Her sincerity shines through and her "just do it" attitude is an inspiration to all who hear her.

I am very proud to know Jean Driscoll, and I'm very proud to be associated with a university that is known worldwide for its consideration of the physically challenged. My good friend Tim Nugent got it going years ago—against tremendous opposition, and the program remains one to be envied.

Chapter 34

Jack Whitman

All of us wonder, from time to time, what might have been. The moment usually passes quickly, erased by the knowledge that God has a plan for us. The plan is often difficult to understand.

Some of us have choices. In my case, I chose to stay in Champaign-Urbana and not to seek a play-by-play or administrative job in a metropolitan area. Could I have made it had I chosen to go? I don't know. All I know is that I had a choice to make, I made it, and I have no regrets. Dennis Swanson and I were at the U of I at the same time and worked on several radio-television projects together. After Dennis graduated, he moved on to Chicago, then Los Angeles, then New York. He became president of ABC Sports. He now runs the NBC affiliate in New York and is very active in the network's Olympic sales efforts. This year he was named National Broadcaster of the Year. I am very happy for Dennis and his family. Could I have done something like that? Who knows? I do wonder about it sometimes.

Others have no choices.

Their lives are changed dramatically, in one moment.

Jack Whitman was an all-around athlete at Galesburg High School. He excelled in all sports, but he loved baseball and football. Despite his size, Jack was convinced that he would someday wear the orange and blue in both sports. And knowing him as I do now, I believe he probably would have.

But he didn't end up having a choice.

Just after Thanksgiving 1949, Jack was charging full speed ahead in Kenney Gym. In his line of sight was a mini-trampoline. He leaped onto the trampoline, but it slipped. Instead of going forward and doing a front flip, Jack went backwards and landed on his neck and back. He was rushed to McKinley Hospital. The news was not good: paralysis.

After major surgery and a long rehabilitation, Jack returned to the U of I in the fall of 1952. His dream of playing baseball and football for the Illini was, of course, over. But as we mentioned previously, if you are in a wheelchair, the U of I is a good place to be.

Whitman made two smart decisions. In 1957, he married a wonderful woman named Jan. She has been his rock ever since. His second decision was to take up archery.

He attacked that sport the same way he did the others. He wanted to be the best. Not just the best at the U of I, not just the best in Illinois, not just the best in the USA, but the best in the world. That was his goal.

He qualified for the Paralympic Games in Rome in 1960 and in Tokyo in 1964.

Competing against the best in the world, the little Silver Streak from Galesburg, Illinois, won thirteen gold medals. Thirteen! He blew them away. Jack was back.

Jack and I worked together for many years after I became vice president and general manger of WDWS/WHMS in 1980. Jack was a super salesman, and I later appointed him sales manager.

We had fun! Jack's sales meetings were a riot as he cracked the whip on Dave Burns, Les Schulte, Tim Battershell,

Stacy Schroeder, Larry Fredrickson, Marsha Silver, Carol Burton and others. He worked harder than most of us, and after a while, I never even thought about him being in a wheelchair.

Jack and Jan are retired now, but the two of them can be seen at just about every Illini athletic event. They attend the games. They go to the booster club meetings. They are orange and blue through and through.

I'm sure there are times when Jack, hunkered down in his chair, armed with a cap, a parka, gloves, a blanket, and other gear, bracing against the icy, swirling winds of Memorial Stadium, watching his team play, thinks about what might have been. But I'm also sure it's only for a moment.

The Turpins love you guys!

Chapter 35

Remembering Dike Eddleman

Teddy Eddleman called me on that Thursday morning. "Jim, will you say a few words at Dike's funeral? He always admired you and listened to all your broadcasts."

Dike Eddleman, the greatest athlete in University of Illinois history, had died the day before, August 1, 2001 at Carle Foundation Hospital in Urbana.

"Of course I will, Teddy. I am honored that you asked me," I replied to Dike's wife and sweetheart. I assumed there would be numerous speakers if I was on the list, but it turned out there would be just three - Ron Guenther, Roger Huddleston, and me. When I thought of all Dike's teammates, friends, relatives, colleagues, and Fighting Illini faithful worldwide who could have been asked to speak, and the fact that Teddy chose me, the pride I felt was overwhelming. So, too, was the task of deciding what to say.

Should I recount his athletic history? Do I talk about his legendary accomplishments at Centralia High School? His eleven varsity letters won at the U of I? Do I talk about the fact that he played in the Final Four and the Rose Bowl and finished second in the Olympic high jump? Do I recall the booming punts, the runbacks for touchdowns, and his Big Ten MVP award?

Perhaps I should look back at his amazing ability to excel when the sports seasons overlapped. For example, two weeks after the London Olympic Games, he was back for his final season at Memorial Stadium. How about the times he would play in a basketball game at Huff Gym, then run down and change uniforms and run through the tunnel that connected Huff and the Armory so that he could high jump for the Illini track team? Oftentimes he would jump 6'7" or 6'8" without warming up and without shedding his sweats.

Maybe I should just read from his daughter's (Diana Eddleman Lenzi) book about her dad and some of his accomplishments:

March 1, 1941: Scored forty-two points against Vandalia, boosting his season total to 751 and breaking a ten-year-old state record.

March 21, 1942: In his final prep game, sank a bucket at the buzzer to lead Centralia past Paris in the IHSA championship game.

June 1946: Helped Illinois win the NCAA track and field championship.

January 1, 1947: Helped Illinois beat UCLA 45-14 in the Rose Bowl.

July 30, 1948: Won second place in the 1948 Olympics.

I was pretty sure that the media would recall these magnificent accomplishments and others in detail between the time Teddy called me and the funeral. I decided to center my remarks on my own personal feelings about Dike and how something very strange happened to me when I got the phone call that Dike had died.

"I was sitting in my living room Wednesday afternoon. The phone rang. The message was: "He's gone." I was not surprised, because we had been following the situation day by day. But suddenly, I sprang to my feet. I found myself standing almost at attention, sort of military-like.

"What had happened? Was this just a reflex or had something, someone, yanked me to my feet?

"After Louise and I talked about Dike for awhile, I began to wonder again: what caused this reaction? Why did I suddenly stand up?

"In Harper Lee's great novel, *To Kill A Mockingbird*, lawyer Atticus Finch had done everything possible to defend a black man accused of raping a white woman in a small southern town. Despite overwhelming evidence that the man was innocent, he was found guilty.

"Immediately the courtroom cleared, except for the blacks who had watched and listened from the balcony along with Atticus's children. As Atticus began to walk slowly out of the courtroom, the blacks began to stand one by one, in tribute to the man. One gentleman, seeing that one of Atticus's children was still sitting down, said, 'Get on your feet, your father is passing by.' Everyone remained standing until Atticus had left the courtroom.

"That, my friends, is respect. Not many people command that kind of respect. It is respect that has to be earned.

"When I learned that Dike Eddleman died, I stood up. Or God jerked me to my feet. A special man had been lost. On your feet!

"A person gathers medals by being a better athlete than the others. Dike certainly did that. We all agree that he was the best ever. And, of course, we respect him for that.

"But the respect I'm talking about is that which is earned by treating us all like kings and queens. That's what he did. All the time.

"Respect is having zero ego when his accomplishments earned him a giant one. Respect is asking every time about your wife, your children, their children. He always said he loved our Christmas card. And always, 'How are you doing, Chief?'

"I see him now, working the parking lots at the football games, getting all pumped up, hoping for an Illini victory. I see him now, coming to the press luncheons, chatting with the media, talking about the upcoming game, having fun. He was just one of the guys.

"If you didn't know who he was, you would never have dreamed of what he did. His heart was so big that it was always close to bursting. And, finally, it did.

"Hey, Ruth, Dempsey, Tilden, Thorpe, Grange, Halas, Combes, Mills, Pace, Eliot, all you champions, on your feet! Dike Eddleman is here."

Section 5

THIS AND THAT

Chapter 36

Fun and Funny

I wish I had recorded all the funny things that happened during the more than thirty years I have broadcast Illini games. Coaches, players, fans, members of the media, and announcers are sometimes very, very funny, almost always unintentionally. Quotes from coaches alone would make an entire book.

When Mike White came to town he was looking for ways to create interest in the football program. As a matter of fact, White turned out to be the best coach-promoter that I've ever been around. He was always thinking up new gimmicks to get people up and into the stadium. Neale Stoner was a great promoter, too. Between the two of them they managed to sell more tickets during the 1980s than Illinois ever sold before or since.

I suggested to White that he should have a football clinic for women. Invite a room full of females, tell them a few things about the game and strategy, show them the equipment the players wear, let them ask questions, provide a few refreshments, and hopefully, some would be hooked. He agreed.

WDWS radio was the main sponsor of the event. We sent out personal invitations, reserved the ballroom at a local hotel, printed a nice program, decorated the room in orange and blue, and waited for the RSVPs. Immediately the replies came rolling in, and on the day of the event there was standing room only—more than 300 women came to listen to Mike and learn some football.

The first thing Mike did was bring out one of our biggest linemen—a real hunk—dressed only in a jock and a pair of shorts. Mike then proceeded to explain all the pads and stuff that players wear, and he dressed the lineman on the spot. When the last piece of equipment went on—the helmet—the crowd applauded.

Mike then asked if there were any questions from the audience. I had a wireless mic in the crowd. Several hands went up. I went to the woman closest to me and gave her the mic. Mike had covered many topics up until then, and he didn't quite know what to expect. The question she asked brought down the house.

"Coach White, do you have those uniforms washed or dry-cleaned?"

When the laughter died down, Mike replied, "I'll be damned if I know!"

Stumped on the first question. It was a moment—like so many others—that endeared Mike White to the Illinois community and helped "put cheeks in the seats," as former ticket manager Mike Hatfield was fond of saying.

Basketball coach Lou Henson liked to hang out in the press box during Illini football games. He loved chatting with the media, and it was a lot warmer up there. Lou was usually attired in normal cold-weather garb, but one day he showed up in the press box with coat and tie, the Lou-Do in place, and shiny shoes.

"Hey, Coach," I asked, "Why are you so dressed up today?"

Lou explained that he was going to be interviewed at halftime by one of the female television sideline reporters.

"But you're a basketball guy. What on earth is she going to ask you during halftime of a football game?" I asked. The coach replied, "It doesn't matter what she asks; I already know what I'm going to tell her." Hard to top that one.

Ed Bond has been the producer and engineer for Illini broadcasts for fifteen years. He has worked for a number of different broadcast rights-holders and is currently employed by WDWS/WHMS radio. Under a separate contract, Ed produces and engineers the Illini games for the Division of Intercollegiate Athletics.

He has developed a sophisticated system of broadcasting the games that is the envy of others who have not yet advanced to the level of the Illini Sports Network. From a technical standpoint, the Illini broadcasts, under Ed's guidance, are second to none. Obviously, this is a big help to the announcers on the broadcast. We are always striving to make sure the content of the broadcasts is equal to the technical side that Ed provides.

Having said all that, there are some things that Ed does that make him a good candidate for this chapter. First of all, his appetite! Ed never starts a game without at least two hot dogs, a giant tub of popcorn, and a couple of soft drinks. All are piled on the floor, under his feet, where he can easily munch on them while never missing a beat engineering. All this, mind you, after Ed has already consumed a pregame meal in the press room or at the hotel.

In addition to kidding Ed about his bright orange pants, which he wears on occasion, we are always on him about the food and his cast-iron stomach. One night in St. Louis at an Illinois-Missouri basketball game, Ed's stomach rebelled.

During the broadcast, I glanced over at Ed, who seemed to be turning whiter and whiter. I could tell something was wrong. If Ed was not there, we would have been helpless. I knew nothing about the equipment, and neither did any of my broadcast partners. Finally, Ed summoned Marty Kaufman, a member of the Division of Intercollegiate Athletics staff, who happened to be sitting a couple of rows behind us at courtside. I saw Ed get up and take off running for the toilet, and Marty sat down in Ed's chair. I continued to broadcast the game, wondering all the while what was going to happen. Did Marty know how to operate the equipment, break for commercials, play the bumper music, and all that? I didn't think so.

The next thing I knew, Marty was on a cell phone getting instructions from Ed, who had taken his own cell phone into the toilet with him. Here we have a big-time broadcast of two terrific college teams on a fifty-station network being engineered by a guy sitting on the john in the bowels of the arena. It worked, and Illinois won!

Ed was so sick that he had to stay over in St. Louis and come home the next day, but he didn't let his illness stand in the way of doing his job. That is true professionalism, but it is also pretty darn funny.

Every Monday night for several years, I hosted the coaches' radio shows. Some were in the WDWS studio and many were at various sites around campus. These shows often produced some very good radio, some very bad radio, some great questions from the audience and phone call-ins, some ridiculous questions from the audience and phone call-ins, some wonderful appearances by football and basketball players, some awful appearances by football and basketball players, some planned fun, and some unplanned fun.

You never knew what to expect from week to week.

With all due respect, many young women at some sorority houses didn't know much about football. If that were the case, the technique used was to provide written-out questions in advance. Thus some young woman who didn't know a football from a hand grenade would ask Coach Ron Turner, "I know that Purdue will throw a lot of different offensive looks at you on Saturday. What do you plan to do to combat that attack?" The question would be followed by polite applause and some nervous giggles from her sorority sisters. Coach Turner, to his credit, would always say, "That's a very good question." Then he would proceed to answer it as if it had been asked by a senior writer from *Sports Illustrated*. He was great at that.

Then another night, we would be at a sorority house where every young woman seemed to know a lot about football and had no need for written-out questions. They would bombard the coach with really good questions of their own.

On one cold winter night at a fraternity house, Lon Kruger lost his voice five minutes into the show. Kruger was always hoarse, and we were always ready with hot tea for him. Usually, the longer the show went and the more tea that he drank, the better he sounded. But this time he was speechless. I was prepared to do the whole show myself, but after stalling for a while and taking questions from the audience and talking on the air to our producer, Dave Johnson, we broke for a commercial. Amazingly, Kruger's voice returned, and we were able to finish the show.

Athletes took part in the shows from time to time. The very best at it was Brandon Lloyd. One night I asked him a question, and he proceeded to take the mic from my hand and start asking me questions. Then he went around the room and started interviewing the audience. I had totally lost control. The audience loved it.

We had Damir Krupalija as a guest several times, always at a sorority house where the sisters swooned when he walked in. At some point during the interview I would do some made-up play-by-play in English and ask Damir, who is from Bosnia, to repeat it in his native tongue. Damir always did a fabulous job and always made sure that no matter what I had said during my play-by-play, his version always had Krupalija making the winning shot.

Johnson invented an Illini Trivia game which we played for a couple of seasons. Two teams would be chosen, the coach would ask the questions, and the participants would try to answer. Most of the time they did a good job, but sometimes it reminded me of Jay Leno's "man on the street" interviews. "What is the name of Illinois' football stadium?" stumped one panel one night. We kept score, and the winners got T-shirts or media guides. It was always fun on site, but I'm not sure how much enjoyment the radio audience got out of it, because they couldn't see what was happening.

"This is Jim, from Rockford," was the way most of our call-ins started, no matter whether it was football or basketball season. Jim was a loyal listener, but always wanted to make a speech before he asked his question. I had to cut in on him several times, but I give him credit for being there every Monday night.

Sometimes we would get a call from a guy who had obviously stopped at the corner tavern on the way home, or perhaps was still in the tavern when he called.

These calls were always funny. As the caller mumbled on and on, I would hold the microphone up to my mouth and tilt my head backwards as if I were taking a swig from a bottle, and the young people loved that.

One thing the coaches had in common: they were always just on time or a little bit late for the start of the show. We started many programs with no coach in sight. Then magically, during the first commercial break, they would show up. Made us nervous, but we got used to it.

During the commercial breaks, the coaches would answer questions that they couldn't answer on the air, most of them having to do with recruiting. I learned a lot during those commercial breaks.

The crowds ranged in size from 150 or so to zero. We showed up at a residence hall one night, I believe it was with Lon Kruger, and there wasn't a single person in a room where chairs had been set up for about 100. We didn't flinch; we just went on anyway and had a terrific show. I interviewed Kruger, and we took phone calls; no one knew the difference, but it sure was strange sitting there in an empty room.

We did the Lou Henson Show from TGI Friday's for several seasons, and it worked out well. Several Illini fans came in for dinner and stayed for the show. The only problem there was the noise and the constant chatter at the bar, which was very close to our broadcast area. When you're at a bar and a young man is trying to have a conversation with a young woman, they have very little interest in what Lou Henson or Jim Turpin or anybody else has to say.

It was March 12, 1987. The place: Birmingham, Alabama. The event: the southeast regional of the Big Dance. The opponents: the Fighting Illini and Austin Peay.

Illinois had just completed a 23-7 season and a fourth-place finish in the Big Ten with a 13-5 mark. Lou Henson's team was the favorite. In fact, Dick Vitale was so certain that Illinois was going to win that he blurted out, "If Austin Peay wins this game, I'll stand on my head, right here in the studio."

Final score: Austin Peay 68, Illinois 67.

It was quite a sight. Vitale on his shiny dome, upside-down, on national television.

Fast-forward to 1989. The Illini are rolling over the opposition in what would turn out to be a season with thirty-one wins. I'm doing a phone interview with Vitale, and I ask him when he's going to come to Illinois and stand on his head. Always anxious to get something going, Vitale replied, "Tell you what, Jim. If Illinois wins the national championship, I'll come to Illinois and stand on my head in the Assembly Hall."

"Dick, that's a pretty safe bet. Only one team wins the national championship. How about this? If Illinois gets to the Final Four, they don't have to win it all, then will you do it?" I countered.

"You got it, baby. If Lou-Do gets his team to Seattle, I'll do it," he said, and the challenge was on.

Vitale loved to call Henson Lou-Do. Some people thought Lou wore a toupee. Lou's standard answer to that was, "If I had a toupee, would it look this bad?"

Well, Illinois did go to the Final Four and Vitale, true to his word, came to the Assembly Hall the following year to do a game for ESPN, and we set up the "stand-on-my-head" bit for the pregame.

I met with Vitale and asked if he was ready to do it. He surveyed the audience and said, "Let's wait a few minutes, there aren't enough people here yet." Always the showman.

A few minutes later, however, he was ready. The cheer-leaders brought out a nice comfy cushion to center court. Vitale emptied his pockets of loose change and then went into a head-stand with flashbulbs popping all around the Hall. With the cheerleaders holding his feet to steady him, he stayed up there for about a minute before yelling, "Jim, get me outta here. All the blood's running to my head. I think I'm gonna pass out." The temptation was to let him. That would have made this story even better. But we let him down, he bowed to the crowd, and the bit was over. The audience loved it.

Now, when I hear Dick on the air and he gets a little too wild-and I'm about to turn him down or off, I remember back to the fun we had with the headstand bit and what a good sport he was, so I leave him on.

Vitale is fun to be around. He knows his role. We all know what he is doing. So everything is okay. I was extremely pleased when he named me to his list of the best college play-by-play men in the nation during the 2001-2002 season.

You can get into some pretty hot arguments about Vitale. Some people just can't stand him. Others love his "dia-per-dandies" and "PTPers" and all the other stuff he throws into a broadcast. I know one thing: if you are doing play-by-play and Dick is doing color, don't count on too much air time that game. Dick will dominate the telecast if you let him. That's his thing: talking. A lot.

I personally think Vitale is great for college basketball. He has the energy and enthusiasm for the game that he con-siders the best of all games. He is a color commentator, coach, cheerleader, and fan, all rolled into one hyper package.

When he walks into an arena there is a buzz that starts immediately. Students, especially, gravitate to him. He passes out his latest book, signs autographs, chats on the court with players and coaches, waves to people in the stands, and eventually gets behind the mic for his broadcast. Vitale is a show himself. But there is one thing that sets him apart from some others: he loves his work, and it shows. And he does his homework. He knows as much about college hoops as anyone, and he keeps plugging away and talking to anyone who will listen, always trying to find out more.

I will remember the 1996 Summer Olympics for lots of reasons, not the least of which is that I broadcast the medal rounds of water polo.

My daughter, Jayne, had worked for the Atlanta Committee for the Olympic Games (ACOG) for four years leading up to the Games. She served as Director of Aquatics for the Games. As such, she had an official ACOG van and a hotel room near downtown Atlanta, within walking distance of the swimming and boxing venues. Our entire family invaded Atlanta and jammed into her hotel room. We took turns sleeping on the bed. Others hit the couch or the floor. It was a great time!

We had purchased tickets to a variety of events, and Jayne had purchased some through ACOG. So we were all set except for track and field, which I wanted to watch every day. I had always been a big fan of track and field and had spent some time with Jayne watching the U.S. trials prior to the Games.

I had no problem getting press credentials for the U.S. trials, but getting them for the Games was impossible. Non-working radio stations are way down the priority list when the requests are coming from all over the world.

Then, my big break!

I received a call from One-on-One Sports in Chicago. They were covering a variety of events and were short of announcers. They asked me if I wanted to do some work down there, and I jumped at the chance, knowing that a press credential would be part of the deal. I would have an entree to events during the entire run of the Olympics. What luck!

I thought perhaps I would be working basketball or track and field or maybe even swimming. When we met in Atlanta, my assignment came as a surprise. No, not a surprise, a shock!   I was assigned to do the play-by-play of water polo!

I explained that not only did I not know anything about water polo, but also that I had never seen a water polo match, or game, or skirmish, whatever they called it.

To make matters worse, the U.S. team failed to qualify for the medal round, and I was left with international teams and international names to learn. This was not shaping up very well.

But when they assigned a former U.S. Olympian to handle the color commentary, things began looking up. As we discussed the broadcast in advance, I proposed that our strategy would be this: I will say that we are trying to educate the uninformed about water polo during the broadcast. My role would be to ask naive questions of the Olympian, just as the uninformed might do. He agreed with that and off we went. I must say that I played my role as "the uninformed one" very well.

We were broadcasting only to those at the venue who had purchased headsets, so it wasn't as if my stupid questions were being heard worldwide. One-on-One Sports gave me a nice check, said I did a great job, and I kept the press credential for the rest of the Games. Without the credential, I would have missed some world record-breaking performances on the track later in the week.

Chapter 37

Top Five Memorable Broadcasts

1. **March 26, 1989:** *Illinois beat Syracuse 89-86 to advance to the Final Four.*
   The game featured several future NBA players on both teams. That was not only the best Illinois team I've ever broadcast, it was the best Illinois team I've ever seen.

2. **January 22, 1989:** *Illinois beat Georgia Tech 103-92 in double overtime.*
   It was great fun shouting, "The Illini are No. 1 in the nation." You don't get a chance to do that very often, no matter how many games you broadcast.

3. **January 28, 1984:** *Illinois beat Michigan 75-66 in four overtimes.*
   I was totally exhausted when this one was over. Beating Michigan is always a thrill, but beating them in this manner is unforgettable. Bruce Douglas played all sixty minutes for the Illini.

4. **1983:** *Illinois beat Ohio State 17-13 on the road to the Rose Bowl.*
   Illinois beat all nine Big Ten teams that season, but that victory-highlighted by Thomas Rooks's great touchdown run was a play-by-play man's dream game.

5. **November 12, 1984:** *Illinois lost to Penn State 35-31.*
   At Penn State, they still refer to this one as "The Game"
   or "The Drive." Although the outcome left me drained
   and disappointed, that game was thrilling to broadcast,
   and I rank it as one of the best college games I have ever
   seen.

   Others that rank near the top: Nick Anderson's shot at Indiana; Dave Downey scores 53 at Indiana; Andy Kaufmann's
   shot versus Iowa.

Chapter 38

The Slush Fund Scandal

The bus began to roll away from our hotel on the way to the United Center for a meeting with Arkansas. The date was December 8, 2002. A few hours later, the Illini would win an ugly one over the Razorbacks, and a few months after that, Arkansas Coach Nolan Richardson would lose his job. The firing and its aftermath were also ugly. Race relations.

But on this day, as the bus proceeded west along Madison Avenue, my thoughts were not on Arkansas, or the House That Michael Built, or even on Bill Self's team. Try as I might, I couldn't concentrate on the business at hand.

I was thinking about another hotel, another game, another Illini coach, another day. It seems that every time I make a trip to Chicago to announce an Illini basketball game, my mind drifts to December 23, 1967: the day the slush fund became a reality, the day that Coach Harry Combes confessed in front of television cameras that Illinois was guilty of handing out small amounts of cash to various players. The day that was the beginning of the end for Coach Combes, his assistant Howie Braun, head football coach Pete Elliott, and several Illini players.

The Illini were to play California that night at the Chicago Stadium. I was in Coach Combes's hotel room that afternoon, along with Frank Schooley, the director of broadcasting at WILL in Urbana, and Art Morse, the man who put together the famous Chicago Stadium basketball double-headers. There may have been others, but I specifically remember that Frank and Art were there, trying to comfort Coach Combes and to give him advice.

Outside the hotel room, several reporters had gathered, all seeking Coach Combes's reaction to the announcement made earlier by Big Ten Commissioner Bill Reed.

Reed confirmed that illegal funds did exist within the University of Illinois athletic department, and said, "These funds were completely apart from the operation of the university's grants-in-aid program. They were created with the knowledge of the director of athletics (Doug Mills) and of the assistant director of athletics (Mel Brewer) and disbursements were made at the direction of the respective head coaches."

As the reporters waited outside the hotel room, Combes argued with Schooley and Morse about what he should do. I recall they tried to tell him not to say anything at that point, "At least talk to your lawyer first, then draft a statement of some kind. Take some time to gather your thoughts."

But Combes argued that these reporters had been friends throughout his coaching career at Illinois, and he owed them something right then and there. Despite protests from Schooley and Morse, Combes walked out into the hallway, and reporters crowded in, television lights blazing.

Combes could have ducked them. He could have stayed in his hotel room. And after he decided to go face them, he could have dodged questions until later. But he didn't.

As I stood in the hallway, pressed against the wall by the crush of reporters, I heard him say, "If we are found guilty, and we are guilty, I hope any punishment would be dealt to the coaches and not to the players. We deserve it. They don't."

The statement was startling.

"Combes Admits Guilt," screamed the headlines the next day. That night, every television station in Chicago rolled the admission-of-guilt clip.

But those of us who knew Harry Combes were not surprised by his candor. He felt he owed a statement of some sort to his friends in the media, and he told them the truth. That's the kind of guy he was. To this day, many people close to the Illini program feel that Combes was the scapegoat in the slush fund scandal. That he knew of its existence, but that he played no role in setting up the fund and disagreed with having it. But no one knows for sure. At least, I don't.

In covering the Illini for more than forty years, I don't remember ever being part of a more dramatic scene than the one that played out that afternoon.

There are those who have discouraged me from writing anything about the slush fund scandal in this book. They argue that I have been part of so many positive happenings and should not "dig up old dirt."

I counter with the argument that the slush fund scandal is as much a part of Illinois athletic history as the championships and the trophies. In addition, more than thirty years have passed since those dark days, and there are presumably vast numbers of Illini fans and faithful who have grown up not knowing many, if any, details of what happened. Let me summarize for those people.

In those days, the Big Ten Conference had a ban on what was called "walking-around money" permitted by the NCAA. The NCAA allowed athletes to be paid $15 a month for laundry, movies, snacks, etc.

The Big Ten was obviously at a competitive disadvantage with the other conferences that permitted the $15 a month.

The Big Ten allowed athletic scholarships that included room, board, tuition and fees–an estimated value of $2,000 a year at Illinois. Big Ten athletes had to sign statements saying that they would not accept unauthorized funds beyond scholarships.

Reportedly, the football slush fund at Illinois was started in 1962 by alumni after Pete Elliot's second Illini team finished 0-9, the school's worst football record in history. The fund was intended, primarily, to meet the complaints of prospective athletes that they could go to other conferences and get $15 per month. In 1964, a similar fund was started for basketball.

The slush fund might have gone on for several years without detection had not it been for plans to announce a new athletic director and a new head football coach in December 1966. Elliott was to become the AD, and one of his assistants, Bill Taylor (who graduated from Nebraska in 1956 and served under Elliott at Nebraska and California before coming to Illinois with him), was to become the head football coach.

These plans did not sit well with Brewer. Brewer, a long-time Illini player, assistant football coach, and current assistant AD, thought he should be promoted to either AD or head football coach. He decided to blow the whistle.

Brewer decided to take the slush fund ledgers, in which he kept meticulous records of income and payments to players, to U of I President David Dodds Henry. Perhaps he thought he would somehow be rewarded for doing this, but exactly the opposite happened. President Henry ordered an internal investigation and notified the Big Ten of the existence of the slush fund.

A Big Ten investigation revealed that Elliott, Combes, and Braun were all aware of the fund and all authorized payments from the fund to athletes. Eventually, the results of the investigation were ruled on by the Big Ten athletic directors. Their ruling was brutal.

"The University of Illinois is ordered to show just cause why its conference membership should not be severed if it retains the three coaches (Elliott, Braun, Combes) on the athletic staff."

President Henry immediately issued a statement saying "the ruling is too harsh for the infractions, and Illinois will appeal to the faculty representatives."

President Henry, faculty representative Leslie Bryan, and university legal counsel James Costello decided to make a three-way presentation to the faculty reps. Henry went to the meeting armed with backing from alumni, the Illinois High School Coaches Association, the Illini football team, the Board of Directors of the Athletic Association, Governor Otto Kerner and many others. There was a strong feeling that Illinois would withdraw from the Big Ten rather than bow to the edict of the athletic directors.

But the faculty reps held firm, and there were strong indications that the NCAA would follow in support of the Big Ten decision. The total athletic program at the U of I could have been jeopardized, and there were no more appeals. So the three coaches offered to resign, and President Henry reluctantly accepted their resignations.

In addition, five Illinois athletes lost all further eligibility, three others partial eligibility, and six were cleared of suspension by the Big Ten.

The basketball team was hit hardest: Rich Jones and Ron Dunlap lost all further eligibility, while Steve Kuberski and Randy Crews lost partial eligibility. In football, Cyril Pinder, Derek Faison and Bob Stevens lost all further eligibility and Oscar Polite lost partial eligibility.

Illinois' next football title would come sixteen years later.

Illinois' next basketball title would come seventeen years later.

Did Illinois break the rules? Yes.

Should Illinois have been punished? Yes.

Did the punishment fit the crime? Are you kidding?

Chapter 39

The Neale Stoner Years

Neale Stoner resigned as athletic director at the University of Illinois in July 1988. Fourteen years later, the mention of his name still heats the blood of both his detractors and defenders. Mention Neale Stoner in a group of people, and a hot argument immediately breaks out.

Wasn't he the right man at the right time for the U of I, and didn't he raise money, build buildings, pack the stadium, and provide much-needed leadership for the Athletic Association? Yes. Wasn't he the one on whose watch the Illini went on probation three times in the 80s, and wasn't he the one whose high-rolling and loose management style sent hordes of investigators scurrying down the money trail? Yes. He was all of that and much, much more.

U of I math professor Bill Ferguson headed the search committee that was looking for an aggressive and experienced athletic director. Neale Stoner's name kept popping up when the committee asked people nationwide to provide them with some hot prospects. Stoner was AD at Cal State Fullerton at the time. Ferguson called Stoner and asked him to come talk with the committee. He wowed the committee from the start, and three weeks later he was hired. For about eight years there was little doubt that the right decision had been made. Then, in the summer of 1988, it all fell apart.

Stoner had led the way as the Illini moved into the upper echelons of the Big Ten conference. Private support for the athletic association and its programs rose to record levels. The football and basketball teams got better and better, and there was renewed spirit and vigor among Illini supporters.

John Cribbet, the chancellor when Stoner was hired, said, "We were looking for a go-getter. We wanted someone who could take charge and turn the program around. He did that, but because he was a go-getter, he stepped on a few toes." Well, actually, more than a few.

As buildings went up and private money poured in, the football team, led by Mike White, put together a string of sellout crowds. In 1983, White's team beat the other nine teams in the Big Ten conference on the way to the Rose Bowl on January 1, 1984. No matter that the team was thrashed by UCLA, the Illini were rolling, and the slogan, "The 80s Belong to the Illini," was no longer just a slogan.

In the midst of all this success, Stoner was neglecting some management duties and some rules. He adopted a business ethic that eventually did him in. The U of I's investigation found, among other things:

- Unsupportable and unauthorized credit card charges
- The use of maintenance personnel and AA equipment for personal reasons
- The use of gifts-in-kind for personal benefit
- The use of AA funds for non-business travel
- Circumvention of bidding requirements
- Serious miscalculations of AA income and expenses

In July of 1987, Stoner fired veteran baseball coach Tom Dedin and replaced him with Augie Garrido, one of several people Stoner brought in from Cal State Fullerton. Garrido, one of the nation's most successful baseball coaches, was given a contract worth $100,000 plus perks. Fans of Dedin were upset. Dedin's top salary as head baseball coach was $37,225.

The following May, Stoner fired strength coach Bill Kroll and replaced him with Leo Ward, who was brother-in-law to associate athletic director Vance Redfern, another transplant from Cal State Fullerton. That decision opened the floodgates for a wave of allegations, some anonymous and some not, centering on maintenance men being used to work on the homes and cars of AA officers.

After a long and thorough investigation into these and other allegations, the U of I decided in July that it was time to terminate its contract with Stoner. Mort Weir, who was chancellor at the time, explained his thinking to Illini supporters this way:

"After weighing the positives and negatives, my conclusion was that he could no longer lead the program effectively and with an overall reputation of high integrity."

Weir went on to say that while the U of I could have dismissed Stoner for cause, that course was not taken because a court challenge was certain. Such a case would have been costly and difficult for the U of I to win, but it was necessary to end the relationship nonetheless.

The uproar among Stoner friends and supporters really got ugly.

A former U of I football player and close friend of Stoner and Stoner's attorney, Dan Webb, blamed *The Champaign-Urbana News-Gazette*.

He charged that *The News-Gazette* was reacting irresponsibly (in leading the investigation in the media) in an effort to thwart a short-term threat to the broadcast rights of WDWS for Illini football and basketball games. (*The News-Gazette* and WDWS are both owned by Mrs. Marajen Stevick Chinigo.)

At one point he phoned me at home and asked, "What's it gonna take to get this thing (the investigation by *The News-Gazette*) stopped? Do you guys want money? Do you want a long-term contract to broadcast the games? What is it you want?" I hung up on him.

He simply had it wrong.

Bill Rasmussen had signed a three-year contract in 1986 with Stoner for the U of I radio and television broadcasts in early May. Rasmussen's company, Rasmussen Communications, held the rights to the broadcasts and then subcontracted the actual broadcasting duties to various radio and television stations. Rasmussen sent me a letter on May 21 indicating that broadcast rights for the 1988-89 season would be open to bids June l.

This meant that any and all radio stations in the Champaign-Urbana market could bid on the games. Presumably, the highest bidder would carry the Illini football and basketball games.

What Rasmussen had forgotten was that I had a signed document (signed by Rasmussen and by me) showing that WDWS had one year left on a three-year agreement with Rasmussen's company to carry the games on WDWS. It took me several days to contact Rasmussen by phone and remind him of the deal already on the books. Rasmussen explained that he had simply forgotten about our deal, and he immediately instructed his radio director, Will Tieman, to call all the stations in the Champaign-Urbana market and apologize for the mistake. There would be no bidding for the radio rights that year because WDWS already had a contract. This was a blooper of major proportions, one of many regarding broadcasting rights for Illini games. Several companies tried to make the radio rights agreement work, but none did until Ron

Guenther later decided to forget the outside firms and take the whole thing in-house, turning it over to advertising genius Bill Yonan.

Although the radio rights issue was a concern to our companies, it was but a brief side issue to what was happening at *The News-Gazette* with regard to Stoner. The *Gazette's* tracking of questionable aspects of athletic department operations had begun at least three months prior. That's when columnist and writer Loren Tate approached editor John Foreman to tell him that a controversial story was brewing.

Tate told Foreman that it had to do with the impending ouster of strength coach Bill Kroll and the apparent intent to move associate athletic director Vance Redfern's brother-in-law, Leo Ward, into that position.

Unbeknownst to Tate at the time, Kroll had talked to state Representative Tim Johnson. Johnson concluded that interviews for the position ran afoul of affirmative action guidelines. Johnson went forward, confronting Stoner with this and another allegation in the athletic director's office.

Tate began chasing down other allegations. Stoner was cooperative with Tate until Tate asked him about his decision to have the Athletic Association pay roughly $2,000 for Redfern's lengthy visit to a weight-reduction clinic at Duke University.

Stoner said he would no longer deal with Tate on a personal basis and asked Tate to put all future questions in writing with copies to the chancellor and the president.

That's the way it all began. It gained momentum with Johnson's involvement.

It reached the serious stage with the "deep-throat" letters that followed and became a matter for investigating officials with the maintenance workers' willingness to talk.

I look back upon the Stoner years with both sadness and joy. There is no doubt that Stoner did some wonderful things for the University that I love so much. It is likewise true that his shady deals and high-rolling lifestyle were grounds for investigation and subsequent resignation and settlement, accepted by the U of I to avoid a lawsuit.

But there are memories of the 1980s that stick with me. Memorial Stadium never looked that good–before or after. That sea of orange, those wacky and wonderful Tailgreat parties and competition among friends and neighbors, the wins over all nine Big Ten teams in 1983 on the way to the Rose Bowl, those pro-type quarterbacks that Mike White brought in–Dave Wilson, Tony Eason, Jack Trudeau, and Jeff George, the excitement that surrounded each game, beginning early in the week, reaching a heart-stopping level at the Quarterback Club meetings on Fridays, and the flood of fans on Saturday. Smiles everywhere! It was fun!

At the same time the football team was rolling, Lou Henson's basketball team provided thrills aplenty. Bruce Douglas led the Illini to a share of the Big Ten title in 1983-84 by winning fifteen of eighteen conference games. The season ended with a controversial loss to Kentucky on the Wildcats' home floor in Lexington.

Mike Hebert's volleyball team, from 1983 to 1994, won 299 matches and lost just 118, a winning percentage of .717. His teams went to the NCAA tournament ten consecutive years, including back-to-back Final Four appearances in 1987 and 1988.

In many ways, the 80s did belong to the Illini. Stoner deserves credit for that.

Chapter 40

Broadcast Rights

In August 1983, for a fee in excess of $250,000 per year over the next three years, Anheuser-Busch was granted a quasi-exclusive right to the radio broadcasts of Fighting Illini football and basketball games by Athletic Director Neale Stoner.

It was to be the first of several such contracts granted to various companies nationwide, as one after another failed to produce the big dollars expected by those companies and by the University of Illinois.

Prior to 1983, several stations originated Illini games. At one time almost all of the booths in the press box were assigned to stations in Decatur, Danville, Peoria, Belleville, Champaign, and others. Veteran broadcasters Sid Rotz of WSOY in Decatur, Max Shaffer of WDAN in Danville, Elzer Marks of WITY in Danville, plus several others, were no longer permitted to broadcast the games as Stoner sought to fulfill four objectives:

(1) Make more money. Under the old system, Stoner felt only a small percentage of the financial potential was being generated.

(2) Stoner was concerned about the quality of the presentation. He didn't like the idea of having a lot of different broadcasters talking about the football product in a

variety of ways. Under exclusivity, Stoner would have more control over what was said about the teams. He hoped the new arrangement would help the Illini land good radio stations in both Chicago and St. Louis.

(3) The new statewide network would have a big impact on fundraising and recruiting.

(4) Stoner saw the Big Ten moving in the "exclusivity" direction by reducing the number of spaces available in press boxes. The freeing up of space in this manner opened those radio booths to donors.

At that time I was broadcasting Illini football games on WDWS and 14 other stations on the Purity Sunbeam Football Network, financed by the Purity Baking Company in Decatur and long-time Illini fan and friend Chuck Webb. Stoner permitted us to keep the network, thus the "quasi-exclusivity" mentioned earlier. But if we lost a station for whatever reason, we would have to try to replace it in that same market. We were not permitted to expand beyond the original fifteen markets.

My main concerns were that our rights fees became larger, and as a subcontractor we were no longer to deal with the Athletic Association, but rather with Anheuser-Busch, on policy matters.

When WTAX in Springfield, a long-time affiliate on the Purity Sunbeam Network, elected to go with Anheuser-Busch, I signed a contract with WSMI in Litchfield, which was listed by Arbitron as part of the Springfield market. This was fine with Webb and Purity, but Anheuser-Busch said no and ruled WSMI off-limits. WSMI owner Hayward Talley protested that he had a contract with me and had the games two-thirds sold. He tried to work it out with Tom Barton at

Anheuser-Busch, but to no avail. Talley was surprised that decisions about Illinois football on radio were being made in St. Louis. At that point no one was very familiar with the concept of corporations owning the rights fees to University broadcasts.

Once the Anheuser-Busch network was set up, that was it. Stations that were not on that network or the Purity network were out of luck. Pittsfield, Kankakee, and others called me and begged to be on our network, but there was nothing I could do.

Anheuser-Busch wasn't happy with our network being part of the arrangement. Their best interests would be served if WDWS would drop its originations of the games and get out of the sports broadcasting business. WKIO was named as Anheuser-Busch's Champaign-Urbana outlet.

But Anheuser-Busch and all the future rights holders overestimated the amount of money to be made. They saw Chicago as a gold mine, only to find that Chicago advertisers and Chicago radio stations weren't much interested in University of Illinois sports. Even today the Chicago outlet for Illini games is likely to bump our games off the air—or place them on another station—when scheduling conflicts arise.

As the years sped by, several other companies gave it a try. Raycom, Rasmussen Communications, Tieman Broadcasting Company, and Learfield Sports all fell short of expected revenue. Some came back to the U of I and pleaded to renegotiate their contracts; others left the Illini holding the bag. Lawsuits were filed, but Illinois never got what it wanted or expected until Athletic Director Ron Guenther decided to bypass the middleman (the rights holder) and move the whole operation in-house.

He hired Bill Yonan, a former advertising executive for Time-Life, to handle the selling. Dave Johnson, who was already on staff, set up the network and worked with the affiliate stations. It worked like a charm. For the first time, the DIA showed a very substantial profit and has been profitable every year since. Yonan has since retired and moved to North Carolina, and his assistant, Warren Hood, took over his duties.

The battle to continue to be the "Voice of the Illini," both as a radio station and as an announcer, has been a difficult one. There have been times when we were very close to losing it all, but we refused to give in. I don't know what will happen in the future, but right now the situation is good, as WDWS/WHMS and the DIA cooperate quite nicely and are producing a variety of quality radio products.

Neale Stoner had the right idea about selling broadcasting rights in 1983; it's a shame it took so many years to make it work.

Chapter 41

Penny for Your Thoughts

In addition to broadcasting Illini football and basketball games, hosting the coaches' call-in shows, and cohosting the "Saturday Sportsline" with Loren Tate, my on-air duties at WDWS include "Penny for Your Thoughts."

"Penny," as most of us refer to it, is a two-hour talk show that runs from 9-11 a.m. Monday through Friday. I have hosted this program for more than twenty-two years. It has been a blast, at least for me. Presumably others enjoy it, too; the ratings are always good, and there is rarely a shortage of callers.

In February 2002, the Champaign City Council voted to designate Windsor Road between Neil Street and Prospect Avenue as "Honorary Jim Turpin's Penny Lane." Windsor Road runs east and west, just south of WDWS.

Stu Meacham, on behalf of the Fellowship of Christian Athletes, submitted the request for the designation. The FCA had hoped to surprise me with the honor at their March 2002 banquet, but the ever-vigilant media picked up the story from the Council's agenda. Nonetheless, I consider the designation a great honor, and I'm very proud of it. It gives me a great feeling to know that my children and grandchildren will be able to see those signs long after I have signed off the show.

"Penny" began as a fifteen-minute program. It was then expanded to half an hour, then an hour, and finally two hours. No one is quite sure when "Penny" was started, but it has been on the air for most of the life of WDWS, and the station went on the air in 1937. During that time, there have been just three hosts: Mark Howard, Larry Stewart, and me.

In the early days, WDWS lacked the proper equipment to get callers on the air, so the only thing the listeners would hear was the voice of the host. The host would talk to the caller, but only the host's voice could be heard. A segment might have sounded like this:

Host: "Good morning, Tom, you're on the air."

(long pause)

Host: "Is that right? How did that happen?"

(long pause)

Host: " Hey, Tom, that's a terrific story. Thanks for sharing it with us."

(long pause)

Host: "That's good, Tom. Say hello to Mary for me."

Then the host would try to recap what Tom had said. Somehow the show survived until the WDWS engineers figured out a way to get both sides of the conversation on the air.

The show is a mixture of guests and callers. Sometimes the show gets bogged down, no one calls, and the host resorts to a monologue. This is my least favorite kind of show.

The guests have included big-name authors, Supreme Court justices, mayors, state's attorneys, lawyers, state officials (including several governors), show business stars, local high school bands and singing groups, and University of Illinois officials, including presidents, chancellors, and professors.

As you might imagine, a show that has run that long sometimes has its unintentional humorous moments. Former U.S. Senator Charles Percy provided one such moment.

Following a very serious interview that lasted an hour, the senator stood up but failed to remove his headset. Guests wear headsets in order to hear what the callers have to say. As he stood up, I could see he was going to have a problem with the headset, so I stood up too, and reached over in an attempt to remove the headset before he jerked the wires out of the console.

Senator Percy, still not realizing what was happening with the headset, thought I was about to hug him. So he reached over and hugged me! It must have been quite a sight: a politician, a radio talk show host, tangled wires, and headsets that slid from ears to noses to eyes.

It was the first and last time I have been hugged by a politician following an interview. (Or any other time, for that matter.) But I did vote for Senator Percy anyway. He was a darn good senator.

Many of the guests are known only by their first names. When a person calls "Penny," we never screen the call. We never ask what they want to talk about. We ask only that they give us their first name, so I can address them to start the conversation.

Thus, we never know what they want to talk about when we say, "Good morning, Such-and-such. You're on the air." This can be dangerous.

Larry Stewart likes to tell the story about interviewing Hollywood star Gregory Peck in the "Penny" studio. Larry gave Peck an appropriate buildup—"great actor, star of dozens of great movies, etc." Then Larry said, "We'll be back with Gregory Peck after this commercial break."

Not much doubt about what was coming, right?

Wrong! Gregory Peck's presence didn't faze the first caller. When Larry welcomed her to the program, he of course expected a question for Gregory Peck. But the caller said, "Good morning, Larry. I have lost my collie, and I'm just sick about it. Do you think you could help me find him?"

For one of the few times in his life, Larry was speechless.

But Peck saved the day. The mighty actor replied to the caller: "What color is your collie, ma'am?"

And she proceeded to tell him. Peck promised that he and Larry would help her find the dog. Larry, still in a state of shock, went to the next caller.

Later, it is fun to talk about those kinds of moments. But at the time, I can assure you that you better be ready when you tell someone "You are on the air," because you never know what's coming next.

One day I was interviewing Dennis Swanson. Dennis was from Springfield, and at the time he was a student manager for Harry Combes's basketball team. Dennis went on to a very successful career in broadcasting and at one time was president of ABC Sports. He is now with NBC in New York and very active in the network's coverage and sales of the Olympic Games.

But that day I was talking to Dennis about basketball. Dennis told me that he had just finished picking his All-Ugly Big Ten Team and wanted to know if I would like to know who made it. "Sure," I said. Who wouldn't want to know the five ugliest players in the Big Ten conference?

He proceeded to name four players, the last of whom was a player from Northwestern who shall remain nameless. Let's just call him "Brad."

I waited for Dennis to name the fifth player, and when he didn't, I asked him why.

His reply was, "Brad is so ugly he gets two places on the first team!"

The next time we played Northwestern, I took a close look at "Brad." And you know, Dennis was right. That kid was ugly!

Then there was Charley.

Charley was a caller who was nuts about education. He was a very smart man and often asked questions that had no answers. And he asked them of everybody. His favorite question was: "What is a quality education?"

I was interviewing former University of Illinois President Stan Ikenberry one day, and Charley called in with his question. "What is a quality education?"

Now Stan Ikenberry is one of the smartest men I have ever known and is respected as one of the leading education authorities in the world. He gave Charley what I considered a wonderful, articulate, well-reasoned reply. To which Charley responded, "No, that's not it." I then asked Charley to give his own answer if he didn't like Ikenberry's. To which he replied, "I asked you first."

In the spring of 2002, we decided to name a "Penny" All-Star Caller Team. The idea was to name six to eight callers, bring them together in the studio for a two-hour, slam-bang, knock 'em dead, anything goes conversation with each other. I would moderate.

To qualify for this powerful forum, each person must:

1. Be a frequent caller to "Penny."
2. Be a caller who has a way of irritating other callers and listeners.
3. Be a caller with "tunnel vision"–your point of view is the *only* POV.

4. Be a caller who dwells on racism, religion, abortion, and the Chief.

    or

5. Be a caller who can out-coach the coaches.

    or

6. Be a caller who can out-play the players.

    or

7. Be a caller who can out-officiate the officials.

    or

8. Be a caller who begins a monologue with one minute to go in the program.

9. Be a caller who complains when he/she is cut off for CBS News. (see No. 8)

10. Be a caller who loves or hates Rush Limbaugh.

The team was not hard to pick.

The captain was certainly going to be Betty. Betty is fond of ending each sentence with the phrase, "you know what I mean?" Most often the answer to that question is, "No, I haven't the slightest idea." Just kidding. Betty may be the only Bill Clinton fan left standing in our community, but I give her credit for keeping up on world affairs and for standing up for what she thinks is right. Betty thinks I don't like her, because I almost always disagree with her.

Don was another first-teamer, selected for his ability to irritate members of the audience on either side of the issue. It is said that Don can walk into a room, spend five minutes mingling, walk out, and those who are left in the room will be arguing without even knowing why.

As I write this, the other members of the all-star team have not been named, and we haven't had the two-hour show with all of them in the studio together. In the meantime, those of you who have no desire to be on our all-star team should keep calling so that sanity has a chance to prevail and important topics can still top the "Penny" agenda.

One of the great enjoyments of hosting "Penny" is being able to pick the people you want to interview, call 'em up, book 'em, and the fun begins. I have talked to hundreds of guests from all walks of life, with a heavy concentration of members of the judiciary, attorneys, law-enforcement people, and officials from local, state, and national government.

I also like to help promote local organizations, particularly those involved in the production of plays and musicals. Frequently members of the cast will come on the show to sing and chat.

I particularly like to interview authors. I am a big fan of mystery and suspense novelists. I have done multiple interviews with many of them, including my favorite, James Lee Burke.

Burke has won several awards, including two Edgar Awards, and has authored more than twenty books, including a long list of New York Times best-sellers. He writes about Dave Robicheaux, a detective who works out of New Iberia, New Orleans, and Baton Rouge.

Burke's books are filled with descriptive and lyric passages along with terrific plots. He is a *writer* first; he just happens to deal in mysteries. He also writes about a fictional former Texas Ranger named Billy Bob Holland who is now a Texas lawyer.

I like the Holland books, but they can't match the Robicheaux stories.

Another of my favorite authors is Tony Hillerman. Hillerman writes about Navajo policemen Joe Leaphorn and

Jim Chee. Hillerman is past president of the Mystery Writers Association, but shuns interviews. I have tried several times to get him on the air, but he just doesn't do interviews.

Others among my favorites are John Sandford, Robert Ludlum, Frederick Forsyth, and James Patterson.

"I loved going to Israel. I found that everyone there was just like me: Loud and obnoxious."

Thus Brian Silverman recapped on "Penny for Your Thoughts" the visit that he and his son took to Israel a few years ago. That is a sample of why Silverman is the best guest I have on my morning show.

Silverman comes on about every two months, and we devote both hours to taking calls and talking about a variety of topics. Brian is a local attorney (a former public defender), a dabbler in politics (he hasn't won an election yet), an avid Cubs, Bears, and Illini fan, an outspoken member of the local cable TV commission (they have some fancy name now, but I forget what it is), and a guy who is bright and knowledgeable on just about any topic that comes up.

And the best part is that he is willing to talk about any topic and give strong, sometimes controversial, opinions on the air.

"Even if I don't know what I'm talking about I still talk about it," he proudly proclaims.

Silverman doesn't have much use for members of the judiciary or law enforcement who agree to come on as "Penny" guests and then refuse to talk about certain topics, hiding behind the "ethics" of the situation.

One time I paired Silverman with Professor Stephen Kaufman, an opponent of Chief Illiniwek. The two of them squared off for what I thought was an informative and entertaining hour of talk radio. Kaufman devotes many hours to developing strategies to get rid of the Chief. He has spoken out in dozens of public forums and obviously comes well prepared to advance his arguments. Silverman, on the other hand, devotes no time to the topic amidst his active law practice. Yet that morning, Silverman more than held his own. His knowledge of the matter was quite amazing to me.

When people call the show with difficult problems they have been having with cable TV, Brian often asks them to call him at his office later. When they do, he will call the cable company himself and try to help the person get the problem solved. That is really a fine public service.

Brian's biggest difficulty is letting the host (me) say a word or two during the show. I get on him about this all the time, and he promises to do better, but he never does. He is like the Energizer Bunny: He just keeps on talkin'.

Brian also has frequent suggestions for me as to how to run my show, and he has frequent suggestions for Stevie Jay as to how to run the station. He has campaigned for years for us to put the Cubs on FM while the Cardinals are on AM.

Brian understands that WHMS-FM is a music station, but he still wants us to slip a few Cubs games in there.

Brian's battle with muscular dystrophy has slowed him down a little bit, but once he gets in the studio that mind and that mouth start to work overtime. He remains a very dear friend and a wonderful talk-show guest. I think he could have his own talk show–something that he suggests to me quite often. But he couldn't handle the pay cut; you know how it is with those highly-paid barristers.

Chapter 42

Chief Illiniwek

The battle to save Chief Illiniwek as the University of Illinois' symbol began eleven years ago in a modest manner.

The woman who pioneered the movement certainly did not appear to be someone who would scare the opposition in a good fight. She was well past her "playing days" and was soft-spoken, courteous, gentle.

Her only weapon that first day was a roll of stick-on badges that said merely "Save the Chief." She sat behind a card table at the WDWS/WHMS tent at an Illini football game, trying to peddle the stickers to pro-Chief fans. She brought along a friend to lend support, and the two of them sold a bunch of stickers and raised a little money to help finance the next step of the process.

She knew this much: the anti-Chief protesters were receiving far too much publicity in the media. She knew that someone had to take a leadership role and fight back. At that time, she had no idea whether anyone else would join her crusade. Sure, they might buy a sticker and slap one on that day, but what about tomorrow?

And what should she do next? She knew there were thousands of pro-Chief supporters out there, but they were not organized and had no plan to combat the anti-Chief campaign. Those who wanted to get rid of the Chief were sending out news releases regularly, holding protest rallies, and manipulating the media in a disturbing fashion.

Jean Edwards waged a lonely campaign for some time. She and her friend, Eleanor Blair, trudged faithfully to the tent week after week. Stick-on badges, bumper stickers, visors, and other assorted items–all trumpeting her "Save The Chief" slogan–were beginning to catch on. Instead of Jean chasing down people to buy her "weapons," Illini fans began looking for her. The movement, tiny and timid, started to edge forward.

U of I students took up the challenge. They formed the Chief Illiniwek Education foundation and planned several events and fundraisers. Unfortunately, when some of the leaders of that organization graduated, the activities slowed considerably.

Obviously, Jean Edwards needed help in her crusade to let the media, the University of Illinois Board of Trustees, and the anti-Chief protestors know that those who love Chief Illiniwek were not going to sit idly by and see the Chief destroyed.

Up stepped Roger Huddleston. He had strong feelings about the Chief. In 1998, he began handing out, to special Chief supporters framed photographs of the Chief, alongside a poem that he composed:

"Centuries back, a noble spirit was born
Honored champion greeting each prairie morn
Inspiring his people, a legend bound
Excellence was the standard to be found
Faithful to his time, his purpose would not wane.
Integrity and honor are his fame.
Love of his tribe, devotion to his own
Loyal to all who call Illinois home.
In victory or the darkest of defeat

Never wavering, leadership complete
Inherited tradition, year to year
Warrior of great esteem who is held dear
Elect for all time, true and worthy one
Kindred spirit for all in years to come."

One of the people Huddleston honored with "The Chief" photo was Jean Edwards. They formed a friendship, and out of that friendship a team developed. This team soon had other staunch supporters, with two deserving special note, Howard Wakeland and Agnes Sims.

On my radio show, "Penny for Your Thoughts," Roger announced the formation of the "Honor the Chief Society and the Tradition for Which He Stands," an organization whose stated mission is to "provide a unified voice for the thousands of students, faculty, alumni, and friends of the University of Illinois that support and value the Chief Illiniwek tradition."

The organization's objective is to share the history of Chief Illiniwek so that people can gain a better understanding of the heritage surrounding one of our country's most time-honored academic traditions. They proclaimed that "when people take the time to learn about the First Nation People for whom the state of Illinois was named and reflect upon *how* Chief Illiniwek is portrayed by the state's flagship university, they are better able to recognize the difference between an athletic mascot and a time-honored symbol of tradition and respect."

The society, with the help of Mark and Julie Herman, a talented videographer/writer, husband-and-wife team, produced the videotape which told the story of both the Chief and the men—and the woman—who have portrayed the Chief for three-quarters of a century. The video was widely distributed and contributed greatly to the understanding of why the pro-Chief movement is so important.

Rep. Rick Winkel steered a bill through the General Assembly in Springfield that said, basically, that Chief Illiniwek *shall* be the symbol of the University of Illinois. Then Governor Jim Edgar changed the bill to read *may* instead of *shall*, which virtually killed it.

The anti-Chief forces continue to label Chief Illiniwek as a "mascot," and always insert the word "racist" in front of "mascot." The pro-Chief supporters insist that the correct term is "symbol" and not "mascot." They point out the differences in the way Chief Illiniwek is portrayed as opposed to the "mascots" at other universities, such as Florida State.

At the end of the day, it doesn't really matter how many people, committees, or organizations are in favor of or opposed to the Chief. I have always been pro-Chief, and I admire those who have put their heart and soul into the battle. But the vote of the University of Illinois Board of Trustees is the only vote that counts. A difficult call, to be sure.

Section 6

OLNEY
STORIES

Chapter 43

Fortune Tellers and Other Olney Stories

There were two fortune tellers in Olney, and both were located on our block. Mrs. Miller lived directly across the street with her live-in boyfriend, Harry Osborne. The other was a black woman whom everyone called Aunt Teeny. I believe she was the only black woman in Olney at the time. The others had to be out of town by sunset. Everybody and everything (including the squirrels) was white in Olney at the time, except for Aunt Teeny.

Both Mrs. Miller and Aunt Teeny drew tourists. Cars were always pulling up in front of their houses, and people came from all around to have their fortunes told. Mrs. Miller used cards; Aunt Teeny read your palm. Or so folks said. I never had the pleasure of having my fortune told by either of them.

Harry was always drunk. He hung out on the front porch with a bottle close by. During the summer, he sat there in his undershirt and drank. When someone came by to have his or her fortune told, Mrs. Miller would try to hide him in the back of the house. One day, Harry came across the street to Grandma Turpin's house and said he wanted to visit her because she was sick in bed. He wandered into her bedroom, and they talked for a while.

When he left, we discovered that the rubbing alcohol bottle was empty; Harry drank it while talking to Grandma. We used rubbing alcohol in those days to give Grandma a massage.

I can't imagine what kind of shape his stomach and liver were in. When Harry died in his sleep a few years later, Mrs. Miller said he had been very sick with pneumonia. We all knew better. After Harry's death, Mrs. Miller seemed to get very old, very quickly. Then she died, too. Such is love and love lost.

Aunt Teeny had twin grandsons who lived somewhere else, but they would come to visit during the summer. She asked my mother if I could come over and play with them, and Mother said yes. We had a great time, climbing the cherry trees in her yard and drinking lemonade. When people came by to have their fortune told, we sat up high in the trees and giggled at them. Aunt Teeny never seemed to mind.

Playing around with her grandsons was the only experience I had with black people until much later. I played basketball, football, and baseball all the way through high school and never had a black teammate. I regret now that I completely lost track of Aunt Teeny and her two grandsons.

Otis Kimmel was a first grader with me at Cherry Street School in Olney. On the first day of school, when the teacher left the room, Otis ran up and kicked her desk. We laughed. Later, perhaps in the same week, the teacher left the room and Otis ran up, unzipped, and began urinating on the desk. There are some things you just never forget.

The Welkers lived across the street from the school, and they had a big, mean Chow dog. As kids walked to school, he would sit on the front porch and growl and strain at the rope holding him back. One day, he broke the rope and ran right at us. His bite tore right through my bib overalls, but I was lucky. One kid was bitten badly and had to be taken to the doctor. From that day on, we took another route to school, and I am still afraid of some dogs.

Our route to school included a trip over the "overhead bridge" that spanned the railroad track. I knew guys who held cats by their hind legs and tried to dump them into the train smokestack as the train zipped under the bridge. I saw a lot of cats hit the train and bounce off; I don't remember anyone ever hitting the target.

There was a railing about four feet high and four inches wide that kept people from falling off the bridge. Art Kurtz used to walk on top of that railing. It was about the scariest thing I ever saw. He was our hero.

The walk from my house at 127 E. Lafayette to Cherry Street School seemed a long way, but it was a walk that was always filled with fun and laughter, just a bunch of guys screwing around on the way to school. A few years ago, on a visit to Olney, I retraced those steps. The walk didn't seem very far this time, just a few blocks, and the fun and laughter were only memories of a simpler time.

Our principal, Mr. Provines, was a paddling fool. He whacked kids' rear ends daily in his office. Minor offenses resulted in a couple of blows; I think ten or twelve were the most he gave to major violators of school policy. One day, a kid threw a little rubber eraser at me. I caught it and threw it back, just as Mr. Provines entered the room. "Jimmie, come with me to the office," he said.

Two whacks on the butt. It really hurt, but I never told my parents, and I guess he didn't either. Today, Mr. Provines would be sued, fined, and/or put in jail. Mr. P was not PC, that's for sure.

Louise and I were married in the First Christian Church in Olney on August 16, 1952. Rev. Earl Zetsche was the minister, and the wedding went off without a hitch. The "fun" began at the reception, which was held in the garage and on the lawn of Louise's parents. Despite the fact that there were no alcoholic beverages, my buddies were wound up!

First they handcuffed me to the wooden handle of a lawnmower, then took off with the key. After the pictures were taken and everyone had a laugh about it, the fun began to wear off. Peggy Roberts's elderly grandmother was not amused, and she promptly found a saw in the garage and began sawing away at the wooden handle in an effort to free me. This too became a photo opportunity.

Luckily for me, and for the lawnmower handle, the guys showed up with the key, and I was released. To tell the truth, it was one of the more memorable stunts I've ever witnessed at a wedding reception.

Later the bride changed clothes, and we headed off for the honeymoon, which was going to include a night in the rockin' town of Paducah, Kentucky, and a brief stay at Kentucky Lake. We roared away in a rental auto and set our sights to the south.

Just a few miles down the road, we began to detect an awful smell. It seemed to be coming from the engine. I pulled into a gas station, and an attendant came running out to see what we wanted. (Remember when service stations actually offered service?) I told him to check under the hood, which he did.

When he raised the hood, he staggered backwards, holding his hand over his mouth and nose. "What in the hell is that?" I had no idea. Then he finally got the courage to look again. "Somebody put limburger cheese on the engine block, and it has melted," he reported.

As I remember, he got out a hose and some cleaning solution and tried to get rid of the cheese, but the smell stayed with us for a few days. The guys were not satisfied with locking me to a lawnmower; they had to do something nasty to the car as well. Creativity! Yes!

We got to the hotel, Irving Cobb, in Paducah very late, and there wasn't any place to have our wedding-night dinner. Finally, we found a really greasy little cafe. What we ate, I have no idea. But I do remember that we both had stomachaches shortly thereafter.

August 16, 1952 ... a rocky start. We celebrated our 50th anniversary this past August.

His full name was Burl Solomon Turpin. I don't think I ever ran across another person with that combination of names.

He was always fighting a weight problem, and he smoked, which probably contributed to his early death at age 50. His doctor never could fully explain to me what caused his death. He was sitting on the stool in the bathroom when he collapsed and died, falling against the bathroom door. My mother called for help, and Koos Bouman was able to get the door open, but it was too late. Dad probably died instantly.

He was being treated for high blood pressure, shortness of breath, and poor circulation. He always carried a bottle of nitro pills with him. Koos was from Holland and a pen pal to my sister Sue. Dad helped him get the necessary papers to enter the United States. He and Sue married, but later divorced.

Dad played in a band for as long as I can remember. He played the bass fiddle, then later the drums. He always sang with the band. The band played numerous high school proms, including mine at Olney. Kids thought it was cool when I could go directly to him and request songs. Mostly, though, he played clubs.

I recall toting the bass fiddle up long, narrow stairways at the Elks Club, Moose Club, and others. At one point Dad ran a club called the Triangle, just outside Olney. It was smoky and loud and there were numerous fist fights when guys got drunk. My uncle, Jim Hockman, helped Dad run the club. When it was closing time, Dad would let me go around and pick up all the whiskey glasses off the tables and the ashtrays. I still remember the smell. My reward was finding loose change on the tables.

Dad always attended my high school basketball games. He always came in just about the time the games were to start. It was a comforting feeling to see him enter the gym. His only advice to me was to "shoot more."

One Halloween two of my buddies, Joy Runyon and Don Watson, and I stole some pumpkins off someone's front porch and attached them to Joy's car, which had the old headlights that sat on the fenders. It was very cool-looking to see the light shine through the pumpkins. The problem was that the people called the police, and of course, the police had no trouble finding us as we dragged Main Street.

The police took us to the city jail, locked us in cells for a few minutes, and then let us go. Dad was not home when I got there, so I had to tell him the next day. I went to the International Shoe Company, where Dad worked in a hot, steamy basement. He came to the window, and I told him about the previous night's episode. He smiled and told me never to do that again, and I promised I wouldn't. I cried so hard.

I don't know what I was expecting from him.

Shortly before he died, he and I were driving around Flora in his station wagon as he peddled Price Mercantile Products. At one point he stopped the car, looked at me, and said, "If something happens to me, promise that you will take care of your mother." I said I would, even though I didn't know exactly what he meant. He must have known that his time was coming soon.

I don't ever remember him saying, "I love you," to me, and I don't ever remember me saying it to him. That is so sad.

We never had any money. Dad and Mother both worked at the shoe factory, but they didn't make much. His gigs with the band paid very little. Often I went with him to visit a man who loaned money out of his house. He would loan Dad $5 and expected to get it back with interest on Dad's pay day. He would warn that bad things would happen if he didn't get his money on time. I was scared of him, and the experience was humiliating. I vowed never to let that happen to me. This was before credit cards, and everyone dealt in cash.

Dad was a Christmas fanatic. I'm sure he spent money that he didn't have to make sure that we all had nice Christmas presents. He and Uncle Jim made eggnog drinks, laced with whiskey, on Christmas day. I got a sip now and then.

On the day I announced my first Illinois football game, a telegram arrived in the WILL broadcast booth. It said, "Good luck, we are so proud of you," and was signed Dad and Mother. I cried. Memories like that are so few, but so special. When a parent dies early a child misses so much. When Kevin Costner finally got to play catch with his dad in "Field of Dreams," I broke up completely. It was a movie scene that touched many males who yearned for–but never received–a strong father-son relationship.

My parents named me Jimmie after my uncle, Jim Hockman. My middle name is Gale after another uncle, Gale Pigg. Yes, Pigg. His wife, my aunt, was named Nellie Pigg. I had another aunt whose name was Eula Fessel, but everyone called her Aunt Dude. I had to be very careful when talking about my relatives to my friends.

So here I was, Jimmie Gale Turpin, who had relatives named Nellie Pigg and Aunt Dude. And, of course, my father was Burl Solomon. Plus, I wore bib overalls. It was a tough hill to climb!

My wife and I have the same middle name. She is Louise Gayle Van Matre Turpin. At one time, we thought having the same middle name was fate–we were meant for each other. Now it's just something we have to explain to people when we sign official papers and stuff.

Our two daughters were not thrilled with the names they got from us, so they changed them. Christy Lynn is now Christine. Jane Elizabeth is now Jayne. Somewhere along the way, I began using James instead of Jimmie. Mostly it's Jim. Jimmie is a cute name until you are about four.

I registered to vote years ago, using the name Jimmie, and never have changed it. Invariably, elections judges, when handing me the ballot, will shout out "JIMMIE Turpin." Heads pop up. "What?" I shrug my shoulders and mutter, "What can I say?" I really should change it officially.

By the way, the woman who didn't like Christy for her name has two children named Carly and Kendall. (Not exactly Mary or Sue.) The woman who changed her name to Jayne named her little girls Jenna and Jordan.

My son, Daniel Scott Turpin, has kept his name and his spelling, which is a tribute to my wife, who argued me out of naming him Dirk. She thought Dirk Turpin was a little slurry–and, as always, she was right.

I wonder, in recent decades, how many babies have been named Burl? How many Aunt Dudes? How many Nellie Piggs? The Turpins are unique, or something like that.

Epilogue

I have always admired the work of the famous Stan Kenton Orchestra and the brilliant harmonizing of the Four Freshmen. The Four Freshmen sang one song that just knocked me out. Here's how it began:

"And so, it's over. Where did the moments go?"

That song is about a love affair. But it could just as easily be describing my sports broadcasting career. A love affair as well.

And so, it's over. Where did the moments go?

It seems like only yesterday that I was doing one record show on AM and taping another on FM, using four turntables at the same time, at WVLN in Olney. My start in the radio biz. Of course it wasn't yesterday. It was 1952. Fifty years ago.

I never enjoyed television very much. I did the state high school basketball tournament on television for the IHSA for several years. I also hosted the coaches' television shows for awhile. But I never liked it. Perhaps it was because I had a face made for radio, as they say.

I love radio. I love being at the games. The thrill of being able to describe what was happening via play-by-play is a never-to-be-forgotten experience. Very few have the opportunity to do it. There are a whole bunch of people working in radio and television sports who want to do the play-by-play for games. It's the ultimate assignment. Not studio work, not pregame shows, not sports talk shows. Play-by-play is it.

I was never very good at providing a bunch of statistics. I think I was pretty good at describing what was happening on the court. I tried to describe every pass.

If a player had the ball, I wanted you to know who was guarding him. If the coaches were mad at the referees, I wanted you to know. If the team was playing lousy, I tried to tell you the team was playing lousy. If the crowd was into it, I let you know. If they were sitting there acting like they were at a symphony concert, I told you so.

In football, the score of the game, the time on the clock, down and distance, formations, who was in motion-I tried to cover that, and sometimes more, on every play.

The passion for it came easy.

You can have a booming voice, high energy, and a desire to do well, but if there is no passion in your broadcast it isn't much of a broadcast, in my opinion.

The passion came easy for me. I love the University of Illinois and its athletic teams. In my heart, the spirit of the orange and blue is there every day.

I can hear Ray Eliot right now. I can see J.C. Caroline and Mickey Bates running over Woody Hayes's 1953 team right now. I can hear the Marching Illini in my sleep. I dream about '89 and the national championship that could have been. I cried when Matt Heldman was killed and when George Bon Salle went ineligible and when they burned the Chief in effigy right outside Memorial Stadium–a stadium dedicated to those who gave their lives so that we can live peacefully and watch our games. Shame on those folks who did the burning at that location.

Now that I am no longer the Voice of the Illini, I realize it will never be quite the same again.

Oh, I will go to the games and sit in the press box (I have a lifetime pass, you know) and enjoy the competition and pull for an Illini victory, but it won't be the same as doing the play-by-play. Time marches on.

People asked me all summer what I was going to do in retirement, now that I had all that free time on my hands. And they asked "Will you miss doing the games?" I hope to continue doing my regular work at WDWS for a long time. That would include "Penny for Your Thoughts" and the "Saturday Sportsline."

Miss doing the games? It has been my life. Of course I will miss it.

I admire our fans. The ones who tailgate and wear the orange and blue and follow the team on the road. And how could we get along without the Quarterback Club and the Rebounders and all the other support groups? We have some great fans, but sadly, I don't see myself becoming one of them.

I know it would probably be the right thing to do to sit in the stands with my family and stand and cheer. Maybe some day, but right now I don't see it happening. Old habits are hard to break. Call me a play-by-play guy. Retired.

It has been a wonderful ride. No one should have that much fun and get paid for it. I have attempted in this book to share with you some of what I have experienced. I have tried to relate–in my own words, I never claimed to be a writer–what it has been like to be the play-by-play voice of the University of Illinois Fighting Illini football and basketball teams for so many years. I hope I have succeeded in some small measure.

Hail to the Orange! Hail to the Blue!
Hail Alma Mater! Ever so true!

Acknowledgments

My first attempt at putting a book together has been both a joy and a pain.

Without the help and encouragement of a lot of people it simply never would have happened. And without the friendship of those I write about, I would never have had enough courage to put their stories on paper. In addition, I want to use this opportunity to thank several people I have met and worked with during my career. This is always dangerous, because some who deserve to be mentioned will be unintentionally left out. Let me apologize for that in advance.

Mrs. Marajen Stevick Chinigo: Thank you for giving me a job more than 20 years ago and for letting me do it. I shall be eternally grateful for the opportunity to work for such a wonderful company, owner, and boss.

John Foreman at *The News-Gazette*: I deeply appreciate your confidence and trust in me. I won't disappoint you.

Ron Guenther at the DIA: Thank you for this long run. I always tried to do my best each and every time the mic went on. I only wish it could have lasted longer.

Stevie Jay and all my colleagues at WDWS/WHMS: I'm proud of our two stations for the information and entertainment that they provide, but I'm even prouder that we do it with class. I look forward to a continuing role as host for "Penny for Your Thoughts" and cohost, with Loren Tate, of the "Saturday Sportsline."

Ed Bond at WDWS/WHMS: Thanks for making me look good on "Penny" and the game broadcasts, remotes, and Monday night call-in shows. Your technical expertise and enthusiasm for the Illini have helped take us to another level on the air.

Loren Tate at *The News-Gazette* and WDWS/WHMS: You have contributed mightily to our sports programming, and I look forward to our time together on Saturday mornings. I think our Saturday show is hard to top. Thanks for everything.

Jeff Ingrum, Stacy Robbins, Jana Perry, Angie Lancaster, Penny Ransom and all the other great people at Health Alliance: Working with you in letting people know about a great product (Premier Choice) has been a lot of fun for me, and I take great pride in what has been accomplished to date.

Dorothy Damewood and Cindy Butkovich in the basketball offices: Your kindness and thoughtfulness to me and my family have been much appreciated. You two certainly made my job a lot easier.

Mary Gallagher and Janann Vance in the football offices: Thank you for all your help with all those different coaches. You helped me more than you will ever know.

Bob Nicolette, Skip Pickering, and Rod Cardinal: You guys were really great to be around, and I will always admire your skills as trainers, but more than that, I'll remember the good times we had together. Your friendship means a lot to me.

Dave Johnson, Kent Brown, Al Martindale, Andy Dixon, Mike Hatfield, Dana Brenner, Cassie Arner, Doug Green, Dick Barnes, Derrick Burson, Mike Koon, Michelle Warner, Vince Ille, Warren Hood, Marty Kaufmann, Shawn Wax, Ken Zimmerman, Chris Tuttle, Cheryl Cain, Tom

Michael, Sue Johnson, Lenny Willis, Mary Ann McChesney, Jesse Ratliff, Terry Cole, Kelly Landry, Marsha Goldenstein and all the others on Ron Guenther's staff: Thanks for everything!!

Susan Robinson, Katie Moore, and Amy Quesse: the Monday night shows on the road wouldn't have been nearly as much fun without you. You provided the spark and good humor that kept me–and the show–moving. Thanks much! And to Kristen Porter: Thank you for launching the sorority house shows at your house. It was a great night and it got us started off on the right foot.

Dr. Robert Gurtler: Those Friday night dinners on the road were very special.

Dr. Steve Soboroff: Thanks for your friendship.

Stan Ikenberry and John Cribbet: You guys were–and are–the best!

Bill Yonan: Thanks for getting the in-house network started.

Jim Grabowski: Hall of Famer, we had fun–even during that 0-11 season.

Steve Bardo: We had such a short time together, but I enjoyed it very much. Good luck to you in your future endeavors. Hope to see you on the big network soon.

Tim Johnson at the Fellowship of Christian Athletes: Thanks for all your kindnesses toward me and my family. Your work is very significant, so keep it up. I know you will. Let me know how I can help you.

Roger Huddleston: Your understanding and guidance through the battles to save Chief Illiniwek cannot be overestimated. Those of us who love the Chief are grateful for your efforts.

Champaign Rotary and Champaign Kiwanis: Thanks for asking me to MC all those banquets. And thanks for your multi-year commitment to the Illini football and basketball programs, respectively.

It is impossible to name and thank all the coaches, assistant coaches, athletic directors, faculty reps, and others that I've worked with. But I must single out Lou and Mary Henson. If there are finer people in this world, I'd like to know who they are. Thanks for your long-time friendship.

Mike Pearson at Sports Publishing: I will always be grateful for your leadership on this project, even if you did move to Kalamazoo right in the middle of it. There would have been no book without you.

Peter and Joe Bannon, Susan Moyer, Kenny O'Brien, Stephanie Fuqua, Cindy McNew, and Jim Henehan at Sports Publishing: You folks really know how to do it. Congratulations on your past successes. I hope this one doesn't drag you down too much.

Mark Tupper, Herb Gould, John Supinie, Gary Reinmuth, Brett Dawson, Bob Asmussen, Fowler Connell, Dave Orr, Ed Sherman, Andy Bagnato, Scott Musgrave, Scott Andresen, Chris Widlic, Mike Cleff, Ron Rector, Gary Childs, Steve Batterson, Bob Logan, Dan Roan, Jim Sheppard, Dave Dickey, Jim Rossow, Jim Ruppert: being with the Illini "beat" reporters has been a great joy. I look forward to continuing that relationship.

Don Fischer (Indiana), Larry Clisby (Purdue), Matt LePay (Wisconsin), Steve Jones (Penn State), Ron Gonder, Bob Brooks, and Jim Zabel (Iowa), Dave Eanet (Northwestern), Fred White and Doug Altenberger (Illinois TV), Ray Christensen (Minnesota), Eric Kaelin (Ohio State): my radio and television friends around the Big Ten–keep up the good work. I'll miss you guys.

Illini Radio Network stations and sponsors: Without you there would have been no network, no games on the air across our great state. Thanks very much for all your help all those years. And, to our good friend, the late Chuck Webb, the president of the Purity Baking Company, who dug deep for years and years to keep our little network going: It won't be forgotten, at least by me.

And finally, thank you, Louise. For everything.

Celebrate the Heroes of Illinois Sports and Events
in These Other Acclaimed Titles from Sports Publishing!

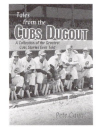
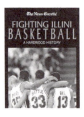